DUBL...
MEMORY BOOK

(Recollections and Stories together comprising a social history of Dublin and Ireland in the 20th Century)

Assembled in

Clareville Day Centre

Edited and Cover Design

by Krunchie Killeen

Memories, of course, can be inaccurate. Dates, names and other details have not been checked, and no claim is made as to the accuracy of matters recounted in this book.

Dublin Memory Book

Published by Clareville Cente Ltd, 2018

© Clareville Centre Ltd

ISBN-13:

978-1981878819

ISBN-10:

1981878815

Clareville Centre Ltd

Glasnevin

D11 R527

Ireland

clarevillecentre@hotmail.com

Available in Paperback in Clareville Centre and on Amazon and other online stores

Also available on Kindle

About this book:

This book is a collection of writings assembled in *Clareville Day Centre, Glasnevin, Dublin*. The initiative began as a competition, announced in the following notice, and was continued after the competition concluded, as well as including one or two pre-existing pieces

---

CREATIVE WRITING COMPETITION

TITLE: My Memoirs

PRIZE €100; PRIZE €75; PRIZE €50
Prize-winning Life Stories will be printed in a Book Format

SUGGESTIONS TO GET STARTED:
(No need to stick to this, just samples. You can use whatever style, subject and format you like)

Childhood days, School Days
Entertainment (TV, Radio, Favourite Band)
First Love, Friendship, First Job
Family Circumstances or Political Scene
Personal Accomplishments, Hobbies
Changes through the Decades: 30's & 40's, etc.
Marriage, Kids
After Retirement.

Quality of writing is more important than the Quantity. You can Read out your favourite Part of your Life Story every Monday, Tuesday, and Wednesday with Ciara, Helen, Linda and Gita. You can give your names to Bridget.

Contents

Killeen, Teresa _____ 7
   Clareville Centre Story _____7

McDermott, Sean _____ 12
   How do you spell "Cat"? _____12

Boland, Bernadette _____ 90
   The Place I would like to call Home _____90
   My Teenage Years in Old Ballymun _____94
   Sudden Retirement _____103

Buckley, William _____ 107
   The Coming of Mary _____107
   Boarding School _____120

Byrne, Sharon _____ 128
   Sharon's Story _____128

Carroll, Nora _____ 131
   From Jamestown Road _____131

Downey, Brian _____ 133
   My Dad _____133

Doyle, Jack _____ 137
   The Golf Ball and other Adventures _____137
   Childhood in the Liberties of Dublin _____143
   The Turkey and Ham _____150
   The Bus Pass _____153

Engledew, Mary _____ 156
   A Varied Life _____156

Ingoldsby, Seán _____ 162

Highlights and Not-So-Highlights of a Young Life	162
Keyes, Pauline	**172**
Never Say Die	172
Killeen, Krunchie	**175**
Big Boys' School	175
One Tea Bag	207
Lyons, Maura	**209**
One Boy and his Dog	209
It's Not All About Money	212
Myers, Patricia	**215**
A Touch of Magic	215
O'Connor, Seán	**249**
Macker	249
Pol Gorm	256
On Infinity in the World	258
O'Doherty, Betty	**265**
Happy Days	265
Oerlemans, Hendrik Jan	**272**
A Sea Captain	272
An Interview with Captain Henk	274
Porter, Mary	**278**
Old Finglas	278
Rickard, Maureen	**282**
A Dublin Life	282
Take Your Time	288
Rooney, Angela	**289**
Our Van	289

Rooney, George — 290
- A Girl Called Susan — 290
- I Got Sacked for Being Santa Claus — 293

Shaw, Ethel Walker — 295
- Mattie and Sammy, the Jack Russell — 295
- The Narrow Door — 301
- The Fate of Fred, the Bantam — 303

Killeen, Teresa

Clareville Centre Story

Clareville Centre is owned and maintained by Dublin City Council (DCC), but is run by a local voluntary organisation with corporate status (*Clareville Centre Limited*).

It is located opposite Glasnevin Cemetery and is surrounded by DCC sheltered accommodation for older and physically-challenged persons: seventy three units in all, seven of which are designed especially to cater for physically-challenged people.

Here is a brief history of the Centre.

In 1980, Claremont Residents Association was the overall winner in the Dublin Tidy Areas competition, and was very interested in the proper development of the surrounding area. It spearheaded the formation of the *Finglas Road Joint Action Group*, which drew representatives from all the Residents Associations in the Glasnevin and Phibsborough areas.

The principal concern of the *Action Group* was the development of a built environment that would facilitate a sustainable, thriving community. The critical impetus in 1980 was the acquisition of the land at Clareville by DCC from the Glasnevin Cemeteries Trust and its plans for the development of the site.

The *Joint Action Group* entered into lengthy discussions with DCC, which resulted in a development that included sixty family houses, amenity open space, and sheltered accommodation for older and disabled persons. This development was completed in 1986 and included a Community Room as part of the sheltered accommodation.

In 1994, another plot of land at the site, which had been reserved for road development, was given over to housing and, following further prolonged discussion with the *Joint Action Group*, which now included representatives of the new housing at Clareville Grove, Claremont Lawns and the sheltered accommodation at Clareville Court, a further 35 sheltered bungalows were completed in 2000.

This *"Phase 2"* included a larger Community Centre to cater for the attendance of approximately one hundred persons, *Clareville Centre*. Facilities were provided in the Centre for healthcare services both to residents of the sheltered accommodation and to other needful persons of the district.

The thirty five bungalows in *Phase 2* consist of twenty four one bedroom single-story dwellings, seven special needs dwellings (having from one to three bedrooms) and two family dwellings. All dwellings and facilities of this phase are accessible to wheelchair visitors. The development is heated by a district scheme, distributed by underground hot mains from a central gas-fired boiler house.

Phase 3 consists of *The Tower Room: Seomra na Smaointe.*

The Management Committee began planning to build a sun-room in early 2006. Approval was obtained from DCC, and the Committee applied to *Pobal* for a grant to cover part of the cost. The application was successful, and DCC put up the remainder of the cost, and agreed to manage the construction.

A competition was run among the service-users of the Centre for a suitable name for the sun-room; and the winning title was adopted as its formal name, i.e., "*The Tower Room: Seomra na Smaointe,*" and it was opened by the Lord Mayor, Cllr Eimear Costello, on 18 May 2010.

The Centre is within walking distance (500 metres) of a large variety of amenities; shops, post office, doctors, chemist, restaurants – at Hart's Corner, which serves as a local focus. All intervening kerbs have been dished for easy walking and wheelchair access.

De Courcy Square, nearby, Dublin's first declared residential Area of Architectural Conservation, contains a community allotment, and *Prospect Square*, beside it, houses a village green in front of *The Gravediggers*, one of the most famous pubs in Dublin.

Glasnevin Cemetery is just across the road, with its new

museum and Interpretative Centre. It is now a top national tourist attraction, and contains a modern restaurant and coffee shop, as well as research facilities and a cosy Church where public Mass is said on Sundays and Feast Days.

A pedestrian, wheelchair-friendly, gate now links the Cemetery to the National Botanical Gardens, making the Gardens accessible to our residents via a ten minute walk.

Many famous individuals who resonate through Irish history are buried in the cemetery, e.g., Charles Stewart Parnell, Michael Collins and Eamon de Valera. Writers and poets include Brendan Behan, Gerard Manly Hopkins, James Clarence Mangan and Zozimus. The parents of James Joyce also rest there. The focal point of the cemetery is the O'Connell Monument, which contains a reliquary of Daniel O'Connell.

Dublin City Centre, with all of its amenities, lies within two miles of Clareville. Another favourite destination for residents of Clareville Court (via 3 stops on the 140 Bus Route) is Phibsborough Village, recently voted in an international survey as one of the top thirty Residential Areas in the world.

In 2015, Clareville Centre took first prize in the *Age Friendly Community Initiative* category of the IPB Pride of Place Competition. The Judges said:

"The winning entry having captured the hearts and minds of the judges showed an excellent caring group of highly committed people from all walks of life. It demonstrated what the judges believe is a model of best practice in caring for the elderly in their own place. Here was shown the attention to all aspects of the older person's needs in a dignified and high quality environment. The emphasis on detail, and on the provision of real opportunities for care-staff to develop their skills, makes this project special."

Teresa Killeen is manager of Clareville Day Centre.

McDermott, Sean

How do you spell "Cat"?
The Story of a Stroke

I

The 10th of January 1999 was a bitter cold day. It was, also, the day that changed my life forever. I had an appointment with a legal litigation eagle in Fitzwilliam Square at three o'clock that afternoon. Fate was about to play a very unexpected part. It was nearly two ten when it happened, as I was walking east along Pearse Street, Dublin 2.

The first significant indication that something was wrong started with my right leg becoming stiff, then my right foot refusing to leave the ground. I was totally dumfounded for a split second, until my upper body inclined to one side giving me the feeling of having no balance. My left arm reached out, grasped a bollard to steady myself, when I discovered my right arm was not responding to orders. An aura of lightness and total numbness enveloped me, as if I was in a cocoon, plus I realised that I was going nowhere fast under my own steam.

At that instant, I knew there was something wrong, but what, I could not make out. I got the feeling that I was embarking on an unknown experience, something new, but at the same time very real. The amazing thing was: I had no feeling whatsoever in my entire body. When I tried to walk, my right foot seemed to be stuck to the pavement. My head felt like it was hovering above the rest of my body. It suddenly dawned on me that I had to do something, plus: do it quickly.

At that moment in time a DART train rattled across the bridge above my head. The sudden impact of noise and vibration produced a reaction of awareness inside me that I was still on planet Earth. Something was telling me that I needed help and assistance.

Looking around me, I spotted a young man in a sheepskin overcoat walking briskly towards me. "Excuse me could you phone an ambulance please."

His reaction was instant. Sizing up the situation, he ran across the road to O'Neill's bar. He returned a couple of minutes later to inform me that an ambulance was on the way. The Good Samaritan stayed beside me until the ambulance arrived. I nodded my thanks because my voice was suddenly not working.

The efficient personnel had me strapped on to a stretcher-type wheelchair quickly, then in to the back of the ambulance. The medic informed me that they were taking me to St. James' Hospital, and we would be there in a few minutes.

Then my memory became intermittently vague. I had no recall of arriving at the hospital, or entering the Accident and Emergency Department. Awareness returned to me within the state of bedlam that was the A and E department of St. James' Hospital.

One would have to see the state of chaos that was occurring, to believe it. I've been inside less rough central

Dublin pubs on a Saturday night. Then reality emerged within me, because they were taking me off a trolley and placing me in a battered old wheelchair from a different era.

It was now 3.30. There I was sitting in the middle of the A and E in an auld wheelchair, totally alone. Questions kept coming and going in my mind: why am I here, what has happened to me, where do I go from here? Am I going to be seen by anyone, or does anybody care?

My wheelchair was on the move again, I asked the student nurse as best I could, "what is happening?"

I was curtly told by the student nurse that they needed the space inside the A and E. The nurse deposited me out at the top of the public waiting room. This uncalled-for shunting did not appeal to me one little tiny bit. In fact, I got the feeling that my stay here was not going to be rosy at all.

Finding myself out in the frantic chaos of the waiting room ignited my mind into an unreal racing state of agitation. Questions that I had no answers for began to flash across my mind. What is the matter with me, and why can't I walk under my own steam?

Weird thoughts were coming and going, but no answers. Then I was getting imagery thoughts. Did people who appeared at A and E receive a new form of LSD to aid them through the trauma of the chaos they would have to endure? Now, another peculiarity was occurring: flashes of light bouncing off the walls of the waiting room.

I was assuming, for the time being anyway, that I had been

given some happy medication on my arrival here.

These pleasantries didn't last long. They changed when a cold gust of freezing air enveloped the waiting room. There were plenty of raised voices and uncalled for remarks being exchanged near the doors. Somebody had left the door open, and the cold air was filling the room with unfettered abundance.

I manoeuvred the battered auld wheelchair around to get a better look at the entertainment behind me. Whoever was causing the disturbance was gone; the security had arrived in force.

Now I could see where my flashing lights were coming from: the end of the waiting room was all glass, which faced a road. The lights of the traffic were flashing around the room. So much for my imagery theory of receiving happiness on arrival in A and E!

I noticed a clock on the wall. It was 7.30. Five hours had elapsed; and I was still in the waiting room with a battered auld wheelchair for company. That this was not good enough flashed across my mind. Now what do I do about it?

At the same time questions were arising in my mind, what am I doing here, and what is wrong with me? Time for action, and some answers were called for right now.

I started to manoeuvre my chariot, the battered auld wheelchair, back towards the A and E, with my feet. I was making great progress until I tried to turn, when it happened. My chariot, the battered auld wheelchair, suddenly rocked, then toppled over, and I, on the charge, was slung out like a sack of potatoes.

I was not defeated yet, so I tried to get up and re-engage, but alas, I could not move. My battered auld wheelchair was lying beside me with its tiny wheels spinning. Try as I might to get up, I found that I could not move under my own steam.

Everybody just looked on initially, then a middle-aged lady was galvanised into action. Getting hold of me from the back, she started to hoist me free of the auld wheelchair. Other people came to her assistance and promptly I was sitting back in the wheelchair.

The amazing result of the topple and thud on the floor: I felt nothing either physical or emotional. It was if sensation and awareness were no longer part of my makeup. I was pushed the last few yards back inside the A and E, and I turned to thank the lady, to find no audible words would come from my lips. My head just nodded thanks instead. The lady smiled and left.

What happened immediately after can only be described as lucid intervals. My memory was going like flashing lights on a Christmas tree. I could remember, and then go blank like nothing out of the ordinary had happened. Memory restored; then nothing. Then I am aware, memory working, only to revert to nothing whatsoever. This was repeating: I can recall, I can't recall.

Then there was a doctor with me asking questions. Moved into a cubical, numerous white coats nodding and talking. I can't hear or understand anything that's going on. The next piece of working memory is being in a ward with all the curtains drawn around the beds.

I am in a bed surrounded by a medical team, then sleep.

II

The next morning I did not have a clue where I was; all I wanted was something to drink.

My next-door neighbour for the night popped her head out from behind the curtains. The young woman, in her twenties, then pulled the curtains back a bit and appeared, wearing a black tracksuit. It had been her attire for the night. Then she bellowed at a nurse that she needed some gear. I sized up the young person's plight straight away.

She asked me "what's wrong with you?"

I replied, "That's just it. I don't know."

Speaking to her was pleasant, since I realized I could not talk the previous night. Now I was speaking, even if my speech was slightly slurred and I had a bit of a lisp.

The ward was coming alive and it wasn't the sound of music. It was a mild form of bedlam.

A young nurse came over to inform me that someone would be coming to take care of my cat and dog in about half an hour. I had no recall of talking to anyone about my pets. The mind was boggling. All I had for breakfast was a couple of cups of tea. I wasn't hungry.

At nine o'clock a man turned up from the DSPCA. He was

reassuring, saying that they would take good care of the cat and dog. I gave him my keys and he asked me to sign a receipt book.

Then another mind-blowing occurrence, my signature was a couple of decreasing anticlockwise circles. A nurse observed this, and the two of them left, talking.

The next hour or so, I was kept occupied by junior doctors appearing, examining and disappearing again. They all said little or nothing at all. The cat and dog man returned and gave me the keys, reassuring me that they were in good hands. I thanked him and, as he was leaving, I got the impression that he was as amazed as I was bewildered.

Then I had the arrival of the consultant and his team of head-nodders. He never introduced himself. They just nodded and talked amongst themselves. Then, as per usual, a quick decamp!

Nobody was telling me anything.

All this was not conductive to my mental state. Everything up to now was making me frustrated and angry, at not knowing what was up with me. Why not have a member of these large medical teams sit down and explain things?

I was starting to get the impression that they don't know. Adding to this: do they care at all?

Lunch came and went. I didn't eat much.

Directly after lunch, on the move again, noticing a sign saying "St. James' Hospital," this reignited my brain to where I was. Into a lift I went, and up many floors to wherever they were taking me.

In the ward, I was allocated a room beside the nurse's station. In my new bed, I asked a nurse what was wrong with me. That is when I first heard the word "stroke," which only led to more confusion within me.

"After you have a scan, it will tell us more. Try to relax. Try not to worry. Everything will be alright."

Then she stated that I would live to be eighty five. Great, I thought, giving out ages now!

Over a day in the hospital, and at last a nurse is explaining things to me. Only I was still confused. A stroke! The serious nature of one had not registered in my mind. In fact, my awareness was not in operation at all. It felt like in, only part of the brain working, limbo.

The next morning, I hopped to the bathroom on my left leg, with the good arm holding the furniture for balance. A porter appeared with a wheelchair, stating that I was going for a cat scan. He asked me if I wanted a blanket, telling me it is cold. I refused the offer. In fact, I wasn't cold, and could not feel anything anyway.

When I was being loaded on my back into the scanner, the science fiction writer, H G Wells', name flashed across my mind. Was I going into the future In thIs modern technology? No such luck! A few minutes later, I was on my way back to the ward.

Now back in the ward I was beginning to get bored out of

my mind, or whatever was left, in working order, of it.

I had gone from hopping on the left leg, to taking a step and dragging my right one behind me, all the time holding onto the wall or a piece of furniture. My equilibrium was not the best as I was starting to find out. A couple of times, I nearly toppled over, which slowed my movement down even further. I was basically left to my own devices, and was starting to get the impression that nobody cared. What was happening to me? Normally an extravert, now was I creeping into a shell?

There was a steady flow of hospital, medical and administrative, personnel, etc., appearing in my room, asking questions and filling in forms, as if one gets cured by bureaucracy.

Then, on the third day, a physiotherapist appeared, with a folder under his arm. After the small talk, he consulted his folder. He asked me to sit on the bed; propped up the pillows behind me, and told me to pull myself up. Arms out in front, touch my knees with my fingers, and lie back again. Do this twenty times and you will be grand. With that, he placed the folder under his arm and disappeared. To the best of my knowledge, he never came back to the room again.

Then I had another visitor, armed with the usual folder, this one had a white coat, which indicated doctor.

He said, "We have the result of your scan. It appears you had a clot on the left side of your brain. That explains what happened to you."

My head was spinning. There were numerous questions I would have liked to ask, but the words did not come. This was a new experience for me: the words were inside my head, but I could not get them out.

Another doctor appeared, with the customary folder. Yet again, I found it difficult to converse with him. The words would not come out.

He then said, "Do you like animals?"

I nodded in the affirmative. He then asked me how I would spell cat.

I paused in thought for a moment, dumfounded.

I said "I can't."

He gave me a serious look and said,

"You can make a letter C, can't you?"

Thinking for a second or two, I shook my head: "No, I can't."

Now it was the turn of the doctor to pause: "Don't worry. It will all come back to you in time."

After the usual small talk, he shook my hand, and bid me good day. When the doctor had gone, I felt a tranquil calm for about a minute. Then the mind started racing, then faster; slowing down and then on to speeds that I just could not fathom.

III

Flashing across my mind were images of recent events from when I was picked by the ambulance, until now. Every flashing image that I was seeing was very clear inside my head, like it was happening again – from under the bridge in Pearse Street, the ambulance arriving, the trip to St. James hospital. No memory of arriving there or entering the A and E, until being wheeled out by the young nurse to the waiting room. They needed the space, etc.

It carried on, right up until "how do you spell cat?"

The next trip to the movies in my head wasn't so clear; this was when the film speeded up. It was like the old projectors when the 35 mm film slipped from its sprockets, usually during a good part of a movie. I was being shown a set of framed images flashing across my mind which I could not make out. That's when I decided to snap out of it and return to living in the now. I felt I needed a drink, but that was not realistic, so I settled for a cigarette.

I got a cigarette and lighter from my locker and set out to find where one is allowed to smoke. This would be the first time that I would be out of my room, on foot. Reached the door of my room without any difficulty, telling myself not to hurry; there is no rush.

I asked a hospital worker where one could have a smoke. He promptly informed me "down the end and turn left at the bottom".

Thanks. Looking at the distance that I would have to travel, it was about twenty yards to the corner. I took a deep breath and set out, telling myself not to rush; nice and steady. Leaning against the wall with my good left side, first thing I noticed was that I would have to pass the nurses' station, which was in a recess on my right. Passing the said station, I took a quick glance to my right; nobody even looked at me. Armed with my new found freedom I carried on regardless towards the end of the passage. I was small-stepping with my left foot, then dragging my right foot up to the left and then repeating it all over again. The corner negotiated, left turn and straight out to a covered passageway.

Along the wall were about ten hard seats most of them occupied by men and women dragging on cigarettes, as if their life depended on it.

"Here, have a seat," came a voice.

I hopped the last few yards. Safely seated, I lit up and puffed away. Three drags later, I was getting a nice relaxed stoned buzz inside me.

Most of them were from the Liberties in Dublin; all had bad chests. I ascertained that the ward I was in was for people with respiratory complaints. I had joined the crowd of smokers in the middle of deriding our great health service.

They got around to asking me what I was doing in hospital. I don't really know; something about a clot on the brain and I can't spell cat.

That got howls of laughter, I didn't mean it to be funny; it just came out that way.

Then I told them about the chat I just had with the doctor. The Liberties' wit took over then. Bet you didn't get a reason why it happened. No! You never get an answer. They don't know.

It went on and on, with nobody on the side of the health service. It got me thinking: where will I get an answer from, like now?

The one positive thing about having the chat, it took my mind away from reality for a while.

Going back to my abode, I got the vibes of receiving dirty looks from doctors and nurses alike. I was thinking that they could let me have a wheelchair, well a loan of one even. I would have to carry on stepping with the left and dragging with the right for now.

That evening, lying on the bed, I went into reflective overdrive. What's it all about? Why did it happen and whatever did occur inside my brain? I can't write, and I'm not able to spell. Where is my good IQ gone to?

Thoughts and words in my head, only when I try to utter the words they don't come out. Right: I'll inform them tomorrow about all this and then I'll get some answers. Or so I thought. The night medication was here. Take this; it's to help you sleep. Take it now; thank you.

I did sleep like a log that night.

I couldn't register that I had a stroke. You don't just get one of anything in this life; there has to be a reason for everything.

Let's go to the nurses' station and get some answers right now. Getting dirty looks on the way, as I walked and dragged myself the ten or so yards to the nurses' station! Great, a nice nurse on duty; and on her own!

"Good morning, can I get some answers please?"

She smiled, "Look, I understand you must feel a bit confused; give me a half an hour and I'll be in to you."

Hobbling back to my room, I felt smugly good, you only have to ask in life and you shall receive.

The nurse turned up inside the hour, saying I will be as helpful as I can with the tiny bit I know about it.

The helpful nurse explained that I had a stroke. Strokes can be caused by a blockage of an artery supplying blood to the brain or a bleed into the brain from a burst blood vessel.

What about my right arm and leg? They don't operate the way they should.

Most recovery is made in the first six months. You can never tell, because everyone is different. It's like life; you don't know what's around the corner. We are learning about it all the time.

I thanked the young nurse, but my head was spinning with trying to take that lot in. Everyone is different, still learning about it, recovery in the first six months. It's like life; you don't know what's around the corner. There was plenty of food for thought; plenty to think about. I know what I'm going to do; have a smoke and think about it. So armed with cigarettes and lighter, I collected my own willpower, for the hike out to the smokers' den.

IV

I was here a week now, a little wiser, but still confused. What I really needed was a prognosis of my situation. It might come today; the consultant is due for his weekly visit this morning. All you have to do in this life to get information is ask, or so I thought. I was ready for the consultant when he should turn up.

They turned up; about ten of them. One started talking to the consultant in medical lingo that I could not understand. This mode of operation was not part of my plans; so, when I tried to say what I wanted to, no words would come out. They were gone out the door like bats out of hell, another chance missed.

The next week was just as boring. I had got more aware, plus walking had improved slightly. Still nobody was coming up with a long term plan for me. There wasn't a short one either, come to think of it.

By the day of the consultant's round, I was eager and ready for any occurrence. The morning was progressing along slowly; I was thinking of what I wanted to say to the consultant, when he should turn up. Lunch time came and went; no sign of the consultant, or any doctor for that matter. Straight after lunch I did my step drag stroll to the nurses' station.

"Excuse me. Is the consultant making an appearance with his presence here today?

The nurse had a suppressed smile on her face, "He might show his face, I'll be able to tell you by 2.30".

I was numb for a time when I returned to the room. Anger and frustration were just a few of the feelings that I was experiencing there and then. The question was now arising in my not-working-correctly mind, what to do?

At 2.30 I went back to the nurses' station and asked is he coming, the nurse shook her head slowly. "Just been on the phone there; he can't make it today."

"That's it; I'm off home now, thanks for all your help."

I was in the room finishing dressing, when the nice nurse came in.

"Are you sure you are doing the right thing? Don't want to think about it?"

"No; my mind's made up. I'm going now."

"I'll walk down to the front door with you. Have you got everything?"

On the way to the exit, I explained to the nurse, sixteen days I've been here and feel like a leper. The treatment I've received or the lack of it. Nobody gives a damn, as you have seen yourself.

The nurse was concurring with me, and asking would I be alright.

I assured her that I would, and that I love a challenge.

After wishing me good luck, we shook hands. I then stepped out the door of the hospital into the dusk of a Dublin winter's evening.

V

I was living in a ground-floor flat at the rear of Capel Street, Central Dublin, about a hundred yards from the river Liffey.

After stocking up in the local shop, I finally arrived home. It was taking ages trying to find the phone number of the cat and dog people. I didn't realise it at the time, but to do the simplest of tasks like finding a phone number was a real challenge. The number that I wanted fell out of an address book more by luck than by finesse. I phoned the cat and dog people. They informed me that it's too late now, tomorrow first thing.

Early that evening, the front door bell rang. It was my GP.

Come in.

Inside the living room, he stated that he had forms to fill in concerning me. When he had filled the necessary forms, he took my blood pressure. He placed everything back in his doctor's bag, then turned and faced me,

"Get yourself another GP."

Then he turned and was gone out my front door in a flash. It didn't really sink in at all, because everything happened so quickly.

The next morning I was reunited with my cat and dog, as

the nine o'clock news was being broadcast on the radio. Just as we were saying hello to each other, the front door bell went again. It was a young lady,

"Good morning; I'm your district nurse."

"Hello, come in."

After the small talk, the nurse stated that she would drop around each morning, Monday to Friday, to see if I would need anything.

I explained about my brief visit from my GP, or, should I say, my ex-Doctor.

With that, she took my blood pressure, saying something about getting another doctor.

The nurse also informed me that an occupational therapist and a physiotherapist would be in to see me in the next few days. I was impressed with the nurse, but, at same time, felt that something was not right. Only time will tell.

A couple of days later, an occupational therapist and physiotherapist turned up together.

The occupational fellow said words to the effect, that I didn't need him at all. The physiotherapist said that there was not much wrong with me.

After less than half an hour, they were gone, never to be seen again.

After they were gone, a cloud of anger was slowly but surely descending around me. These so-called professional people were experts at making excuses, so as not to get involved.

Even with my damaged brain from recent events, I was getting the impression all is not well.

That evening, reflecting over the last few weeks from whatever happened inside my head on that day in Pearse Street until the present time, I was certain about one thing, that the health service left a lot to be desired. These last few days: I would not have believed it if I had been told it. The truth was that I had lived it.

Now there was a deep anger festering inside me and I sensed that I could not stop it. Something was telling me that, if I wanted to get through this lot, it was a time for no prisoners. It was impossible not to think about it, because I was living every second of it. I didn't have a clue what to do next but I was not going to be a pushover, that's for sure. Then getting serious about the extent of my injuries; what did I know about my new imposed disabilities? Now I can't write, not able to spell and my awareness is up the creek. That's what I know about, is there more I should add to the list of can-not does? I did know for sure that I was fifty three years old. So, how is one supposed to feel, when you have had something happen inside your brain?

The one outstanding thing about what was happening, or, should I say, not occurring, was that I had approached the nurse about not having a doctor. As far as I could make out, the people that were employed to assist for this sort of event were not interested in my welfare at all. This theory was really proved when, a week later, the district nurse didn't come any more.

There I was left with no doctor, no nurse or anybody medical to aid, assist or explain things to me. Still I only had a stroke, maybe I was not sick enough to warrant any help.

In the next few week's I had become aware of two deficient traits: not being able to interact with any degree of confidence, plus not able to pass oncoming pedestrians on the street, I simply stepped aside and let them pass.

My cross-terrier dog had difficulty coming to terms with this very modest pace. I only had two walking paces slow and not very quick. Soon I was not able to take the dog at all, because my equilibrium was beginning to fail me, especially in a crowded street.

The next venture was to try to seek a new doctor. This was proving to be a whole new challenge, especially when the third doctor I approached was giving me dirty looks before I had said a word.

Then someone suggested that I should go to my area Health office; it's their responsibility, I was duly informed. So up I went to Croke Park the next morning, which housed my area's Health Board offices. I wasn't given the red carpet treatment, all I got was civil service waffle, plus I should do this and that.

On the way back home, I bumped into the person who suggested that I go up to Croke Park in the first place. I informed him about my wasted journey. He retorted, "Get back up there and demand to see someone in charge, and lay down the law to them."

With my new-found zestful advice, I got a taxi to Croke Park that afternoon. "Get into the mind set" was the order to myself. I was determined, this time, not to be messed about.

After telling the young woman at the desk my tale of woe, and letting her know about my displeasure with the whole set up, I asked to see someone in charge. Five minutes later, a nice man appeared and he had a smile on his face. You don't get many happy faces in these places. I revealed my story to him and could not believe the positive vibes that I was getting back. Come back in a couple of days, and see if I've got something for you. On the way out, who do I meet coming in the door? It's my ex-doctor who had got rid of me.

"Hello!" A look of horror appeared on his face. "Looking for a doctor are we," as I walked past him.

I now became aware that it was now late April when I made my way back to the Health Board offices in Croke Park. The Hogan Stand, where the Health Board offices were, was due to be demolished in the near future. The staff were packing up ready for moving out, in the next few days.

Happy face appeared, smiling as usual. "I think that we have a doctor for you."

He excused himself, and returned with a piece of paper. "Doctor, address, telephone number, you have to book an appointment, so give him a bell first thing tomorrow morning. Best of luck; he's a good doctor."

I thanked him, as I shook hands with him.

There was a feeling of elation, as I seemed to be floating out of the soon-to-be-no-more building, having been without a doctor for nearly three months. At the same time I was thinking that I won't be using these narrow stairs anymore. Shortly the building will be empty and, in the near future, it will be no more. I felt a little sadness; still nothing lasts forever.

VI

First thing, the next morning, I booked an appointment with my new GP. It was for the afternoon. I made sure that I was there before my appointed time. My name called and I was directed down a passage to his surgery. He rose to his feet and shook hands with me and as the two of us sat down, he got straight down to his chosen profession.

"I know a small bit about you and that's only what I got in a phone call from the Health Board. I will be your doctor and am prepared to take you on as a patient. "

That's great, I thought. Then he stated that he would take my blood pressure.

"It's a bit high; you will have to go on medication for it. I want you back here in a week; have to keep an eye on the blood pressure. Look, I don't know anything about brain injuries; all that I can tell you about is that numerous things will happen to you, that you won't understand. The only thing you can do is: don't even think about it, let it go. Is there anything that you would like to say to me?"

I could not think of anything to say at that moment. My brain was trying to inwardly digest what the doctor had said to me.

"Good! See you in a week's time."

I thanked him.

Sitting in the park opposite the doctor's surgery, it felt like a large dark cloud was beginning to shift. There was plenty to muse over, but one statement kept recurring, - the doctor saying, "I don't anything about brain injuries."

My head was racing. If a competent doctor doesn't know about brain injuries, then who does? Well at least I've got a proper doctor; an individual that one can talk to.

Rain drops were starting to fall; time to move on; a shower; it was April.

A week later, back at the doctor's, blood pressure still high. It could take some time to get your blood pressure normal, the only thing we can do is keep an eye on it. I am increasing your dosage, come back in a week's time again. Thank you again.

The following week it's still high. All we can do is increase the dosage again.

It was all way over my head; I could not comprehend the seriousness of high blood pressure at that moment in time.

"Doctor what cause's high blood pressure?"

"That's a very good question. We don't really know. I like you back in a week's time."

I thanked him. This brain thing is getting more baffling from one day to the next. Now there's another spanner in the works; high blood pressure.

Hang on, didn't the doctor say there will be numerous things happening that I would not understand, the first day I met him?

I don't even think confused is anywhere near how I feel. Still we are not to wonder why.

The next week was nearly an action replay.

Then the doctor reassured me not to worry, "I will get your blood pressure stabilised."

I asked the doctor would it be possible for me to see a Neurologist.

"I'll write off to James and see what I can do for you. Leave it for two week's this time. Thank you."

Two weeks later, back in the doctor's surgery again. While taking my blood pressure, the doctor relayed to me that he had sent a letter off to the neurologist in James. The blood pressure is still a bit high, but it has dropped a small bit. Can you stay on the same dosage? See you in two week's time.

Thank you again doctor.

An action replay two weeks later, with the exception the dreaded blood pressure was down. The doctor stated we have got it stabilised at last, now to keep it that way. Stay on the same dosage and I will see you in a month. Thank you.

Soon after, I got an appointment with a female neurologist in James' hospital for a couple of week's time.

The big day arrived, so off to James in a much more relaxed state than the last time I was there.

The lady neurologist had a sort of east coast American accent. Lady Doctor was very niggardly with her words, so I decided to have a go.

"Could you please tell me what caused the stroke?"

"High blood pressure!"

"Can I have some physiotherapy?"

Writing on a folder on her, then looked up.

"I've organised six sessions with a physiotherapist; you'll be sent a letter notifying you when they are."

"Thank you."

 Silence! Time to decamp!

Dumfounded again, I departed from the hospital.

So: high blood pressure was the reason for the stroke. Only they don't know what causes high blood pressure in the first place.

Numerous things occur that you won't understand.

You're not joking! Why is there not a book about all this?

Talking about books: I tried to read one a few weeks ago. I had forgotten the first sentence as I was reading the second one. Book-reading deferred until later date. Mind you I was informed: it will all come back to me. All what?

I received a letter from a female physiotherapist in James, with an appointment card.

On the given day off to James, all keen and eager!

In the waiting room, name called. It was a female with reddish hair. I'll be your physiotherapist while you attend here. Then she states, I have talked to the neurologist that gave you these sessions, you know. Thinking: how could I know?

This is one very important physiotherapist that I've got here. I wonder if she is in love with herself?

I better watch out. In the gym she had me walking up and down, telling me how to walk. Then, on to the exercise bike, where I started off alright. I quickened up a bit, when she bellowed "Watch, watch it, we don't want you having another stroke."

I was put back walking.

"Same time next week;" as she handed me my appointment card!

The next week, the very important physiotherapist wasn't there. I had a replacement – another female. I found her a lot easier to work with.

The following week, the important one was there; worse luck. The next week she, the important one, was somewhere else. On the last two sessions, she was there.

I did not benefit a great deal from the physiotherapy. In fact, it was a complete waste of time.

My head and limbs seemed to come from two different bodies. The mind wanted me to walk in the normal way, but the right side of my body did not respond to orders.

Fatigue was affecting me. Also, I could not understand why it was happening.

Another characteristic of my make-up was not being able to sustain focus on anything for any duration. This resulted in having to find new modes of doing things that previously I could achieve without thinking. It gave me the feeling that there was a blockage somewhere in my *doing-things* system.

Doing normal tasks was energy-draining, which led to enforced catnaps morning, noon and evening. These period's of catnapping led to me not being able to sleep most nights.

The one sad thing about all this was that now I was finding it very difficult looking after my cat and dog. I arranged for the D.S.P.C.A. people to take them into care. They gave me an assurance that they would find good home's for them.

The sun was shining when I was doing my usual slow walk down Church Street, where I encountered a TD getting out of his car.

"Hello, what happened to you, I noticed you walking with a limp?"

I said, "If it only were as simple as that!" Then I revealed to him the whole saga so far. He listened with intent, and then explained that he had a meeting to attend right now, asked for my phone number. Then told me he would be in touch tomorrow; sorry to see you like this. I had known the TD for years and found him genuine.

The next day, true to his word, he phoned me.

Would I be home just after five o'clock? I confirmed that I would. He asked for my address.

It was nearly six o'clock when he arrived. I relayed the whole story, with all the main players in the mind-boggling real life drama to him.

Leave it with me and I'll get back to you. Within a week he was back to me, I've organised a meeting with all the principal people involved for two weeks time.

The TD couldn't make it to the meeting; he sent one of his staff instead. The meeting took place in some government office in Mountjoy Square. Those attending the meeting were mostly health care senior staff, plus my own doctor. All that was coming out of the Health Board people was self-justification; and it was my fault anyway. They were relating to James' hospital, about me dragging my bad foot behind me.

What should I do, carry it?

The whole thing was geared up to concur with the Health Board being right. There were numerous recommendations made, which my GP witnessed, and the meeting broke up.

Being inexperienced of the adverse situation in the health service, I thought things would get done. Yes, by Christmas, but which Christmas? One recommendation was implemented; that was only done because I chased it up.

All this time, I had no feeling in the right hand side of my body, plus I was quite impaired with regards to doing anything.

VII

After talking to a few people, I decided to obtain a transfer from where I was living. I knew someone who worked in the transfer section of Dublin Corporation. I made an appointment to see her in the City Offices on Wood Quay. After meeting her, I was introduced to the senior welfare officer. Between them, they set the wheels in motion.

I transferred to a sheltered housing complex in *Clareville Court*, Glasnevin, not far from the cemetery, in the spring of 2000. It is lovely and quiet, plus it much conducive to my needs. At the same time I still wasn't aware of what damage had being done or what I should do to rectify my disabilities.

I did know that my feelings and emotions were switched off. Even though I was having a lot of turmoil through what wasn't being done, or not knowing if I could do anything myself, I had no feeling whatsoever in my body. It was like being numb, wrapped in cotton wool and feeling somewhere else.

At times there were twenty thoughts a second flashing across my brain; and it was confusion, on top of more confusion.

I lost my balance numerous times, falling over, but never felt a thing. The bruises I only came aware of at a later date. I was not aware some of the time that I had fallen. It was only when I noticed the bruises on top of older ones, I realized that I must have fallen over. Between all this my brain was constantly racing ahead and there was no relaxation at all. It was like livings in a twilight zone of go, and carry on going.

My doctor informed me that, since he had been my GP, he had sent nine letter's to different sections of the Health Board. There was nothing done, he never even got an answer. The GP said to me that the Health Board had failed me. It was all down to myself to survive.

One thing that did happen, when I moved to Glasnevin, was that I was supplied with a male home help. He was fantastic, even though he supported Manchester United. Still, no one is perfect. One could not heap enough praise on him. I started getting around more, with my home help's prompting and encouragement.

With more mobility, some feeling started returning to the right side of my body.

I had noticed other traits beginning to function again. Awareness and emotions were coming around again, not great but an improvement to where I had been. The phase of being an unwilling introvert was slowly diminishing. There was a few psychological and neurological changes happening. On a positive note, I had feeling and awareness returning. There was a negative side also; anger was beginning to raise its ugly head. I still felt there was more positive than negative traits happening overall. It was like going down a track I'd been on before.

I woke up one morning in violent pain, on the right side of my body. This was new to me, so I made an appointment with my doctor. The doctor didn't understand this any more than I did. He gave me a prescription for pain killers, but told me not to get fond of them.

I took them for two days, the pain abated and it never bothered me again. It was replaced by an awareness of stiffness, in and around my right limbs. This was like: every action has a reaction. I don't know; but I did know at that time there was plenty of action going on inside my head.

With feeling returning, a higher sensitivity was now operating throughout my entire body. This also helped my awareness of things that I couldn't put my finger on. There was so much action inside the head, I would need a computer to keep up with it.

Even with positive events happening, there was now an awareness that I couldn't speak correctly. At times I had trouble starting a sentence. I had got into the habit of using the F word to aid me to begin anything I wanted to say. There were times I did not have to use my unconventional method, the words just flowed out.

Then it was suggested to me that I should get in contact with the Central Remedial Clinic, (CRC), in Clontarf. A person came out to see me. I explained the situation as best I could to him. He stated that what they could for neurological issues was limited. I went out there two days a week.

There was transport to and from my front door. It was a new psychological boost for me. By this stage I was virtually a captive in my own home. My first impression was amazement at the size of the establishment. There was a great deal of positive action around the entire building. Disabilities did not bother young and elderly alike. They were darting around the place, some of them in electrical wheelchairs, along their separate paths of life. What really struck a chord were the permanent smiles on young people's faces.

After going there for a month or so, I was more compatible with time and the duration of time. It was then I got the inclination of being more aware of time and how to use it to one's advantage. You can't improve your ability to do anything better, if you are in a rush to achieve, or, in my case, to re-learn everything again. I was thinking more about relaxation, which would be an aid to slowing down. There was a bit of a snag at the same time. I didn't know anything about relaxing or how to go about it.

It was now two and a half years of inactivity. I was game for action, but didn't know how to get things started. Since I had started going out to the CRC, there was a rebirth of awareness, life and time. It was like my brain was being re-born. I could not select one single fact at being the impetus of living with disability. This place certainly helped.

I still had the problem of mobility to contend with, being dependant on the good nature of people, some of the time, to get around. After talking about push-bikes to a neighbour, and how to go on one again, she told me to have a go on hers.

I had to mount the bike with one hand gripping the handlebar, the brake pulled tight and the other hand leaning against a low wall just to mount it. Once aboard I thought: ready – push off with one foot firmly on the pedal and the other anchored to the ground. So I pushed with the foot on the pedal. I was moving! The other foot came off the ground to engage the other pedal, to play its cycling role. Both hands were gripping the handlebars firmly, without letting go.

As I was moving, I was thinking: so this is how one cycles!

Slight elation with my new-found exercise; well I can do it!

"You can cycle," shouted the woman who owned the bike.

My balance on the bike was alright, even though I knew that my equilibrium was not all that that it should be. That's it: my own bike is on the way!

At the same time, one afternoon, in the CRC, I was asked if I would like to take part in a relaxation class. I agreed to give it a try.

They played weird relaxation music, with a commentary telling everyone to relax. I relaxed so much, that I fell asleep. I was thinking: you're not meant to sleep. The weird music was a big turn-off for me. It was only after, while chatting about it, someone said about using classical music to relax with. I made a mental note: that's it – classical music. It has to be better than that weird relaxing noise.

I asked a friend to drop me up to a bicycle shop in Ballygall, just up past the weather centre on Washerwoman's Hill. There I told the owner what kind of a bike I would like because of my disabilities. I gave him my phone number. About a week later he phoned me, to tell me that he had one. So up I went, paid for it, and off I went to tackle life with my new form of transport.

There was a sudden rush of independence as I cycled down the road and on to Washerwoman's Hill. Still going down-hill and passing the weather centre, I had a great feeling of utopia as I gathered pace. Back to reality when the bike reached the bridge over the river Tolka at the Botanic Gardens! I was discovering that one has to peddle to keep the bike moving. Now that I was going up a slight incline, I was peddling like fury to keep moving. How do you change gears? I had to stop to compose myself, and think about it. Then when I had worked it out, off I went again. Being totally unfit and not a lot of strength in my legs, it was hard work to begin with. Pity, they don't design route's that go down-hill; period. Never mind the hard work, the elation of the found independence, was the predominant factor. For the first time in two and half years, the feeling of being alive did return to me, from the day I got the bike.

Everything went well for about a week, with my new-found independence. The state of new-found utopia vanished as I was nearing an establishment in Glasnevin. I was going too quick and not balanced correctly, when I pulled up in a hurry. This resulted in me toppling over and banging my right wrist on the ground. After a few choice words, I got up, dusted myself down and back on the bike. I thought nothing more about it, until eight o'clock that evening. The pain in my wrist imploded, just flashed up unbearable. I phoned the doctor. A locum turned up. He took one look at it and gently prodded it a few times. He said, "See that swelling, you must have a small fracture".

An ambulance arrived and took me to Blanchardstown Hospital. They x-rayed the wrist, put it in plaster and gave me an appointment in a couple of days' time. On my return I was x-rayed again and shown where to queue for the orthopaedic consultant. I was eventually called in to see a doctor, a charming individual from Eastern Europe. He said, there's a small fracture in one of the bone's inside your wrist. Keep the plaster on and I'll see you in three weeks.

The plaster didn't stop me riding the bike. In fact, I was becoming quite apt with my new freedom of movement. Stopping and starting were the outstanding danger points that I had to be aware of.

Monday three weeks, I was back in Blanchardstown Hospital. It was also the men's singles final at Wimbledon; it had been carried over from the Sunday because of rain. Firstly, they cut the plaster off my wrist, with a dangerous looking tool its head spinning at a rate of knots. While waiting for the x-ray, I heard one of the staff remark that the consultant was Croatian. Goran Ivanosivic was one of the contestants in today's tennis final. I was called into the surgery at eleven o'clock. Good morning! By the way, the Wimbledon final has been brought forward; it's starting at twelve thirty. Right, first things first, your wrist is fine. You don't need any support on it now. Thank you for telling me about the tennis, I've four patients left, then it's off to watch the tennis. Ivanosivic won Wimbledon in a classic final.

VIII

Prior to the stroke I could operate the basics on a computer, using the word processor to write a letter, etc. Now I didn't know how to switch one on, never mind operate one. Different people were attempting to re-educate me. I was doing grand with the person teaching me staying beside me, encouraging me. Once I was on my own, the memory just didn't function, as well as a complete lack of confidence.

It was back to basics; with the tried-and-trusted ball-point pen. Where, at first, I had trouble gripping the pen, I had developed a new way of holding the pen. The next problem was getting the wrist relaxed enough, to get the mobility back in the hand. After getting all that off to a suitable fashion, there was still the problem of spelling. I could not spell the easiest of word's like, why, when, where, how, this, that, them and so on. So I kept a dictionary handy to look up the simplest of words. The next snag I encountered was that I didn't know the alphabet between E and X. So, I had a pad with the alphabet A. to Z. written down, with the vowels underlined. This helped me greatly. The more I did, the more apt I became. When I thought I was flying, I soon found out that I wasn't. For, if someone said something for me to write down, I could not get a picture of the word in my head, as if I didn't have the knowhow. A way of coping with my problem was see the word first, before attempting to write it down. Gradually with a mixture of perseverance and repetition I discovered that I had just enough to do the basics of spelling and writing.

As to having to start from scratch all over again, I was still going to the CRC twice a week. My right limbs were still giving me trouble in walking and general movement. Then it dawned on me that I needed the help of a physiotherapist, sooner rather than later. I contacted one of the physiotherapists there, only to be told that she was going on maternity leave. Once she had returned from maternity leave, she would be in touch with me.

While waiting for the physiotherapist to return from maternity leave, I was feeling that I was not getting any benefit from the CRC any more. It was as if I needed something more challenging to fill my needs. Even though I didn't really know what my needs were, it was as if I had to do something else.

The physiotherapist returned from maternity leave, to inform me that because of her workload, she couldn't accommodate me there. Then she told me that she would get in touch with the stroke clinic in Baggot Street.

A few weeks later, I received a letter from the stroke clinic in Baggot Street, with an appointment for an assessment. On the allotted day I went over there. That was the day I met this young lady physiotherapist for the first time. I signed certain forms for her, so she could get medical records released. After giving me a physiotherapist's physical, we had a chat about the forth-coming treatment. I was more than impressed with the physiotherapist, who seemed to know what needed to be done. There was no beating around the bush with her. My disabilities were explained to me, and how to correct them.

I had got into the habit of using my right limbs the wrong way. It was easier both psychologically and physically to do movements with my right limbs the wrong way, rather than do it right. The damaged part of the brain got bad habits as well. For the next six months or so I was attending the stroke clinic every week. Within a few weeks, one couldn't but be impressed with the physiotherapist, who was so professional and reassuring with her knowledge. I was re-educated in how to walk the right way i.e. put the heel on the ground first. Think about how you will move, before you do move.

There was a twofold benefit from the sessions of physiotherapy: I was being re-educated in how to move again. I could feel the brain ticking over as I went along. Secondly, there was the benefit of starting to think in a positive fashion – for the first time since that January afternoon in '99.

This gave me more confidence, plus awareness of doing things again.

The thinking was a new introduction to me all over again. After a few weeks, I felt confident enough to cycle across to Baggot Street, even thought I wasn't sure of a suitable route to reach there. The first time going across the city was an experience in itself, especially around Westland Row and Merrion Square area – from taxi-drivers in a hurry to irate van-drivers shouting at all and everything. One has to watch out; a cyclist could be easy prey. After a few trips I found the most direct route that could be used with confidence, away from barking lunatics-in-a-hurry drivers. It was a five mile cycle each way; and I was beginning to really enjoy the journeys there.

My whole body needed re-aligning; it had been pointed out to me that my trunk was listed to one side. When it was first pointed out to me, in the stroke clinic, my initial thought was a moving human, akin to the leaning tower of Pisa. The right steps to counteract the problem could be easier understood than dealt with. It sounded an impossible exercise at first, but, when relaxed and thought about, it can be done. Good physiotherapists are not out to see you suffer, but to aid and help you. It was while attending the stroke clinic that I heard the name Headway mentioned for the first time. The physiotherapist spoke highly about it. I didn't do anything about it then, but I wrote the name down for future reference.

I also learned there that, with the physical workings of the body, came improvements of the mind. It was nearly three years since I had done any proper exercise. One who is recovering from a trauma, the last thing he wants to get involved with is physical exercise. It's only when it strikes home inside yourself, that you realise all the positive qualities that physical exercise gives you in return.

The exercises I was shown in the clinic had to be repeated over and over again to get results. Even though I couldn't feel that I was improving physically, I could sense an aura of approval from the physiotherapist. There is no easy path to recovery.

Then, I was looking for new ways to relax, when classical music was mentioned to me again. After obtaining a couple of classical CDs, I started using them while I was doing my physiotherapy exercises. I found that once I got used to them, it was very relaxing. That's when I came to the conclusion that, if the mind is happy, the body will function better.

Now, when I heard the word "acceptance" being used in various medical establishments, it got me thinking: "What are they on about? Accept what?" I was wondering if it meant "expect?" That thought was dismissed very quickly, I asked this nice district nurse,

"What does acceptance mean when it's used by medical people?"

The retort was: "Accept what has happened to you. Then, and only then, will you start a better recovery."

That's it: I accept.

When I heard the bit, "better recovery," still I wasn't totally aware of the full extent of what acceptance meant.

After attending the stroke clinic for over six months, it was now time that I was moving on. The physiotherapist told me to keep up the good work and to phone up if I find anything troubling me.

I thanked her.

What a difference that physiotherapist made to me in six short months. Her knowledge and skill deserves gratitude of the highest award. Thank you.

Soon after finishing in the stroke clinic, I was thinking what to do next. Plus I was doing some reflecting, since that January afternoon. Told in James' that physical recovery only comes in the first six months; then, at home, told not much wrong with me. All the time some well-meaning people willing to help and advise, but mistakenly; they haven't a clue about brain injuries. Some of the individuals being paid to treat people just couldn't care less. Then, on the other side of the coin, the professional people like the staff of the stroke clinic, who really do care.

I realised that I hadn't done any proper reading in the last three years. The main reason for this was that I had no short- term memory at the time. Added to this, I was finding it very hard to stay focused for any length of time. I started to read the newspapers, short stories and reports at first. My chain of thought wasn't the best either. It improved a little with perseverance, all the time remembering not to do too much.

My thoughts were that, with other things up and running for the better, reading should pose few problems at all. How wrong I was. Improved results in other functions didn't have a knock-on effect in regard to reading. So I returned to the drawing-board, or, in my case, learn-again reading room. This is the way I started again. Get myself in a relaxed mode, and then focus what I wanted to read. Then slowly set about reading, never in a hurry. Then some time after reading an article, I was finding out that I had forgotten parts of it. I carried on in this way, for some time. My reading improved gradually and felt reasonably confident doing it. After what I had experienced, I started taking nothing for granted, plus always having a positive outlook.

At the same time I was doing a daily schedule for relaxation and exercises. I would get up early in the morning, to do my physiotherapy session. All the exercises came from what I had learned in Baggot Street. This took roughly twenty minutes, I then relaxed, sipping bottled water for about five minutes. Then I had four or five sessions of about five minutes duration, with upper body exercises. I didn't need any leg work; I got that during the day on the bike.

I still fell over from time to time, but luckily the falls were less frequent with the improvement of my awareness. Now with feeling returning to my body, I seemed to have a better sense of being. I was thinking back a few years when I could feel nearly nothing. Then I became more focused all round, with the body's definition improving. I had learned to take my time with everything. It was like: the more aware I became, the more I was enlightened to move on to the next stage. With relaxation and slowing down, I was rediscovering different emotions. But unfortunately, anger and frustration came along too. Anger took precedence over anything I was doing to the extent that I would have to take time out and then compose myself until the anger-bout subsided.

The amazing thing about it was the quickness with which it

would occur. Then, once I returned to a composed state, it would go, like it never happened.

Again my GP's words would ring in my ears: "there will be many things that will happen that you won't understand."

Another thing I found it hard to fathom, how suddenly it would take over my system for no reason at all. It was like a repressed emotion that was coming out to show itself after years of being switched off.

When the anger subsided, I found that any frustration went also, like it was on a parallel track with it some of the time. The sensitivity of the central nervous system meant that it needed very little to set it off. Sometimes nobody or nothing would ignite it. With the frustration thing, it never seemed to be contented, what did it want?

The weather is always a topic for conversation. It's also a phenomenon the right side of my body knows about, since feeling returned there. When I had no feeling in my body, I couldn't understand how on some days there was a tightness on the right side of my body, whereas on other days it was nice and loose. With feeling returning I became more aware that the weather has a great deal to do with it. Any day when the air-pressure was low, the muscles in my right limbs would tighten up. If the air pressure was high, my right limbs would be nice and relaxed; no tightness whatsoever. My right limbs were acting like a built in barometer.

There was so much effort being put into repairing the physical parts of my body, I had being ignoring the emotional side of things. From what I could make out, all this was food for anger and other traits.

The repairing mind did not need the extra hassle. At the same time, there was an immaturity of the mind creeping in. On occasion I would have immature responses to things. Added to this, I still had an impediment to my speech. With all these different reactions in the mind, I found the best way to slow down was listening to classical music. It invariably helped soothe the system. Classical music was medication for the mind.

Added to this I couldn't be in a crowd for long, this also applied anywhere with too much din occurring. I could only go to big department stores early in the day; I couldn't stand the noisy, claustrophobia of a packed shop.

IX

I made contact with Headway's head office in Parnell Street. Shortly I received a letter back from a young lady, with an appointment for an interview. We met firstly in Headway's head offices, then up to the offices of the rehabilitation board in North Great Georges Street. This was another positive chapter in the saga of recovery.

I started going to Headway's day centres, firstly in Donnybrook, then out to Clontarf. One of the first things I learned, attending Headway, was their collective naming of brain injuries, ABI: three letters that translates to Acquired Brain Injury. ABI: a person is not born with it, but acquires it along the path of life, through accident or assault, neurological illness or stroke.

At first it does not sound much, but, when one digs deep, you find a never-ending subject of getting few answers. Headway is funded by the Health Board. It's made up of men and women dedicated to trying to understand, plus to aid as best as possible, people who had the misfortune to receive an acquired brain injury.

Now it was getting on for four years since I received my acquired brain injury. It can be very difficult to tell anybody how you really feel. I could now only relate to people who had endured something similar to what I had experienced. That is how I started to begin to understand the unsolved enigma that makes up acquired brain injuries.

Myself; I was not content to sit still and let it happen. I really wanted to do something about helping myself, but where does one start? Questions with unfathomable answers! Still one can only try, with no assurances of success. I told myself to wake up: that is life anyway. There was this feeling that I could do a lot better, physically and neurologically, but was not clued up on the latter.

Another facet that I couldn't fathom was having these eruptions of anger, for no reason at all. I had this feeling that any progress I made, there had to be a price to pay. There was one thing that I did know: negativity was just hanging around the corner, if I faltered in any way. I was also aware, that I couldn't speak properly. Some of the time there was a delayed slur and other little predicaments. There was also a deficiency that I couldn't pronounce words correctly. Other times having the words in my head, but had difficultly expressing them. It was as if the words were in my larynx, but didn't want to go any further.

Everything seemed to be more complicated than it really was. There had to be answers to all this, but it was trying to get any kind of solution. It didn't help either because I was going through a period of extra sensitivity, to touch, sight and sounds. Was it Lord Byron who said "in solitude when we are least alone." My healing head was making sure that I was not alone.

Another thing that I was now really aware of was that the definition of the body had improved after all the good guidance in the stroke clinic. What seemed an impossible task less than a year ago didn't now. Now things were much better; and it improved my confidence no end. I now knew how to walk in a proper way, though not quickly.

X

On New Year's Eve 2002, I was getting ready to go out for the evening, when I felt a little light-headed. Then my right leg didn't want to move. My instantaneous thought was,

"Here we go again, is this a repeat of four years ago"?

I quickly phoned for a doctor. While I was waiting for the doctor to arrive, there were all sorts of weird thoughts flashing through my head. Then suddenly a calmness came over me, as I reiterated the words of my GP when he said to me on the first day I met him, "I don't know anything about brain injuries. There will be numerous things happen to you that you will not understand. Try not to worry about it."

It's a great piece of reassuring medical advice that a doctor could give under the circumstances.

The doctor turned up inside half an hour. He was a locum. I sharply told him the symptoms and how it happened. He took my blood pressure. It's a bit high. He took out his mobile phone, made a call.

While he was waiting to get through, "We better get you to the Mater Hospital and get you seen to."

 On the way to the Mater, I could hear the festivities already taking place. Arriving in the Mater, I handed over a letter, which the Locum had given me. The receiving female doctor took one quick scan of the letter. I was placed on a trolley and connected up to monitoring machines. In no time at all there were two, then four, then six doctors inside the cubicle.

This all happened inside the first hour. They were in and out every couple of minutes, talking in medical jargon. I hadn't a clue what they were talking about; it was all double Dutch to me. It was all making sense to the doctors.

Within three hours a plastic tag was placed around my wrist. A female Chinese doctor said, "We are admitting you, I'll just go and secure a bed for you."

It was now nearly eleven o'clock. The first casualties of the drinking brigade were arriving. I couldn't see them, but could hear them. I was too preoccupied to bother about them; my head was going ten to the dozen. What is wrong this time? Maybe it's blood pressure; no, it can't be, they didn't say. Then what is it? Maybe they don't know.

I was getting all this; then I thought for a moment, "I'm not getting all this, I'm giving all this. Shut up then," telling myself, "all I can do is go along for the ride."

It was moving-house time again; and I was going to the top floor. The bells were ringing, as my trolley came out of the lift; it was a New Year.

My right leg wasn't moving, so I was given a hand into bed. There was no energy left in me, I was asleep in no time. I woke needing the bathroom; and I was in the toilet before realising that I couldn't walk the night before. Getting back into bed, I told a nurse about me being in the bathroom, where last evening I wasn't able to use my leg.

A Manchester bookie was in the next bed to me. He was about forty; he said his heart was missing a beat. I said,

"What happened? Too many favourites get in?

Even though it was New Year's Day, the vampires were around taking blood off patients. Nothing of note happened to me on the first day of the New Year. On the second, the bookie from Manchester got his missing beat sorted out, and off he was back to England.

A doctor belonging to a new neurological team came to see me. He stated that the neurologist would be around to see me tomorrow. I was talking to him, when I asked him what happened that caused the latest whatever, in this never-ending saga?

He said, I'm not telling you.

I left it, thinking "you don't know either."

Then I was taken for a scan, so they could check the inside of my head out.

On the third day the new neurologist came around, a dapper well-groomed gentleman. Just talking to him made a lot of sense. Then out of the blue, he says

"By the way, you know that four years ago you had a bleed inside your brain."

"That's news to me; it's the first I've heard about it."

I was a little taken aback.

"What about the latest episode?"

"The scan shows nothing; it's just one of those things."

We were talking away; there are a few more tests to do.

He shook hands with me, saying he would see me again.

The vampires came around first thing in the morning; they took about five lots of blood off me. Later that morning I was taken for an echo sound; this was a new one on me. After taking off my shirt, a young lady fixed these electrodes with jelly to my chest. She got me to relax, facing a computer monitor; switched it on, and, hey presto, on the screen in front of me was an image of my heart pumping away. You could see all the connections to the heart, with the blood flowing.

I noticed lumps and other things flowing along with the blood. The blood seemed to be moving at a rate of knots. I asked the young lady how long does it take for your blood to travel right around the body. About a minute! Going back to the ward, I couldn't help thinking about all the flotsam going around my system at speed. There and then, I said, "that's it; no more smokes for me. I'm cured."

The next day the neurologist returned; very understanding, as ever. Then he made a statement:

"The only people that really understand brain injuries are the individuals who have got acquired brain injuries."

He also informed me that he had booked me an appointment with the speech and language department.

The following day, I was approached by a lovely junior doctor. She informed me that they were putting me on warfarin, to thin the blood out. After giving me a booklet, I was told, "read this, anything you don't understand, just ask".

Don't miss the smokes, not one bit; I think that echo sounder was a shock to the system. I was getting the feeling that my taste was already improving. I began to relax and feel more at ease about everything; whatever happened on New Year's Eve was over and done with.

The next day I was told that I would be going home later that day. I was talking to the doctors and some medical staff in the ward about New Year's Eve. The only response I got, was "we'll never know." Then on the eighth day, I was discharged.

XI

After being in the Mater, I had a complete re-think regarding diet. Plenty of roughage in the morning, then snack lunchtime, with fat-free dinner in the evening! Plenty of fruit and bottled water!

Shortly afterwards, I got a letter from a speech-and-language therapist in the Mater.

The therapist was from North America, a very easy person to get along with. When we started, the therapist got me to relax, before attempting to talk the way she wanted me to speak. Then: to focus on what I was going to say. This worked quite well up to a point, I was speaking the wrong way, for four years now and if takes time to readjust. As fate transpired, the American lady moved to a hospital in England.

A couple of weeks later, I started with another female therapist. The lady was from Europe. Efficiency and straightforwardness were just two of the new therapist's positive traits. After seeing her for only two weeks, the therapist stated to me that she could see the reasons for the imperfections in my expressive talking. She went on to explain to me how speech worked in the human body. Then she explained to me that I was still in my head with regards my speech. The correct way is that I should be delivering or uttering the words from my larynx, and not my head. With this new found knowledge in mind, I practiced on my own until I improved it. Then I got it up to near perfection over a period of months. I started listening to classical music while I practiced the uttering of words out loud that I wanted say.

There was a saying I used in order to perfect the practicing of words: RELAX-----FOCUS----DELIVER.

This worked for me; it took me over six months. I am sure that in my case, after being shown how to correct the imperfections in my voice and adding classical music, it did help soothe the mind.

Anger is a trait nobody wants. It can appear from anywhere, time or place; comes when you least expect it, and for no reason at all. It doesn't wear off, or go away; in fact it can get worse, as in my case. So I decided to do something about it.

After asking around, I got an address and phone number of a counsellor in Coolock, North Dublin. An appointment and an introductory meeting were arranged with the counsellor.

The bike got me out there; it was a round trip of ten miles. He was middle aged and very easy to relate to. I found him very helpful, but didn't realize the full positives until later. I went for about four months and I really began to enjoy the weekly trips out there. The weather was great that late spring. It was another facet in life that I was being educated about.

When it was coming up to my time of finishing, the counsellor said words to the effect:

"I've counselled many people but I'm amazed, I've been seeing you for four months now, I still don't know what makes you tick".

To put him at ease I said to him you should see it from this side. He said I was an enigma and he couldn't work me out. As we shook hands he gave me three relaxation CDs that he had made up himself. He advised me to practice relaxation as much as possible. If I feel that I would like to return at anytime, I was reassured with the words, "just give us a bell."

Then the words of the neurologist resurfaced:

"The only people that understand acquired brain injuries are the people who have them."

These few well-meaning words began to make a lot of sense, especially where I was coming from. It was now four and a half years since the initial impact; the neurologist's words had inspired me to a new dawning. That's, when I realised that one has to re-educate one's self all over again. Somehow I had to get a positive mindset and, in turn, acceptance of what had happened seemed very important as well.

The GP sent me for a blood test for cholesterol. The result was just over five. He placed me on medication for the cholesterol. It's not gone through the roof, but we'll have to watch it all the same. I cut all fatty foods at the same time.

Things were beginning to look up, overall. I was having better results regarding cognitive values; concentration and memory were much better. Knowledge and perception were coming back to a working fashion. The emotional side of anger-management seemed to be getting better. There appeared to be very little frustration and I had begun to learn how to cope with stress.

At this stage, what I had learned in the last six months was invaluable to a person with acquired brain injury. I'm nearly convinced that recovery is programmed. It is something I had to endure myself, trying to understand everything. I also had come to realise that nobody is or can do the hard work for you. It has to be done by yourself.

My tasting of food was back to normal again for the first time in years. It was like being reborn again, only this time with a taste. I wonder what I had done without it. This was all to do with the brain mending. I was starting to understand again the meaning of being healthy. With my new diet and cycling every day, there were positive benefits in that I was suffering less with fatigue.

To a fashion, I had become more relaxed, less argumentative, plus more aware of all round well being. Self-confidence was getting better, it was like having more assurance. This I wasn't aware of a year ago. I also became more aware of the importance of relaxation. What worked for me was taking time out to listen to classical music. I used to do sessions, never more than an hour.

Before long I felt a sense of rejuvenation. The head was telling me that I needed further striving challenges. Cycling got easier and better

I started going on midweek and weekend breaks all over Ireland. These gave me the impetus of restoring confidence and getting my communication skills working again. With the gradual restoration of confidence, it was a further facet of feeling better.

Another negativity that had entered the equation from time to time was harbouring imaginary fears. I found, in the long run, that it was mind-over-matter; and learnt to ignore them. Anytime they cropped up after that, I was aware of them. I just put it down to negative thought and sent them packing as quickly as they came.

I tried the same with anger and frustration; and attempted to dismiss them as quick as they came. This turned out to be hard work with these two traits, because they had extreme ways of coming back and snapping at you. The more aware I became, the easier it got, because I knew what to look out for.

Regarding general knowledge, I used to have an answer straight away prior to my stroke. The answers were still there; now, however, I found I had to dwell in thought slightly. Sometimes the answers were there, but would not come out. Even though there was an improvement from where I had been, basically I was having to learn everything again. Relearning takes time and can't be rushed, just like a brain healing.

XII

I wasn't attending Headway in Clontarf any more, when I got a phone call from Head office in Parnell Street. Would I like to go on a digital camera course in Lucan, County Dublin? I agreed to take part.

The course was only to last three months, coming up to Christmas '04. Interesting enough though the course was, I never got to grips with it. The reason that I never got the hang of it was quite simple; I wasn't ready for it. Even being willing to take part in it, I was finding out that from now on, I had to be *ready* for anything I took part in and really want to do it.

Prior to the Christmas break, I got another call from Parnell Street, asking me if wanted to attend Coláiste Íde, in Finglas. This was to take part in a Headway Voice Rehabilitation programme. This was due to start in the New Year. I agreed to attend.

At the start of the New Year, there were several letters to and from the Headway staff in Coláiste Íde with me. The correspondence was explaining, what Headway's voice rehabilitation programme was all about. Firstly, they wouldn't have asked you to partake in the course, if they didn't think you were up for it. Hence the programme comes into play at this stage by providing transitional rehabilitation, thus promoting a holistic approach. Then the programme aims to recognize the complex, cognitive, behavioural, social, emotional and medical problems faced by people affected by acquired brain injury and their families.

This practical educational approach identifies the strengths and shortcomings of the individual, while taking on a person-centred approach and incorporates these findings, devoting suitable adaptive compensatory strategies. Then, full training is given to encourage the promotion of using these strategies habitually, as this is a central core of brain rehabilitation, while also promoting a greater insight into the effects of the individual's brain injury.

The rehabilitation activities are designed so the participants will engage in activities related to their particular difficulties, within safe and supported environments. Tasks may include social activities, vocational activities and practical living skills as well as recreational activities. From where I was coming from, I was already aware that one had to learn how to live again. I could see that this rehabilitation programme was designed to help anyone in my position.

The thought of starting in Coláiste Íde was something new and exhilarating to look forward to. The course was an ongoing programme and I was asked to start in February. I thought the end of January would never come, so I again found myself reflecting on occurrences since that afternoon in Pearse Street in '99 when all this kicked off.

For the first two years, I wasn't sure, at times, that I was on planet Earth. Everything seemed to be unsure and indigestible, as in a permanent haze that went on for an infinity. When I moved to Glasnevin a year after the stroke, I was at that period at my lowest ebb. This went on for over a year, leading to depression, which I didn't realise at the time.

At that moment in time, I couldn't see any future, or hope of an improvement from where I was then. That's when I started to build up a friendship with a family of feral cats. These feral cats who have an amazing built-in survival kit, could be an example for anybody that was down in the dumps. There was a mother with two young kittens who were about every day, before long I was feeding them. They would come around most days; and, before long, it was every day. That's when I started to observe the antics of our furry mates. They are never in a hurry unless somebody is chasing them. Look and look again, is another trait that is built-in for their survival. They always seem to have time to spare, because their relaxed aura gives them time.

Over a period, their relaxed state gave me an idea: if the cats can be laid back, why can't I? This was a time when my head was anything but relaxed. So the seeds were sown about relaxation and in finding ways to switch off. I had to think of my local feral laid-back, cats. Thanks cats! Those two kittens are now over six years old.

Finally, the big day arrived in Coláiste Íde, Finglas. Day one was just "getting to know you" and all about the regulations. One thing I did find from the offset was my communication skills, or the lack of them. A person would introduce themselves to me, but, inside a couple of minutes, I'd forgotten their name. I'll have to have a word with my furry friends in Glasnevin.

The headway staff there consisted of three ladies who were great, more than helpful, with a zest to get the show on the road. One of them I called "lady with the infectious smile," another "lady with intellectual eyes," the other, "lady sister," because she used to be a nurse.

Travelling to Coláiste Íde, I used the bike except on foul-weather days. It was a bit of a push going there, especially if there was a north wind blowing directly into your face.

Returning from there, it was practically all downhill, and I could be home in ten minutes. For the first time since the stroke, there was a serene theme about life all of a sudden:

who needs hassle?

I was under no illusion; there was plenty of flotsam in my brain that needed jettisoning. On the recovery route, I had learned that the brain has over sixty thousand thoughts a day, of which eighty percent are negative. I'm trying to devise a plan to stop them entering in the first place. It was a hopeful desire to further my recovery when I started in Coláiste Íde; to find proper and suitable goals, to advance from day one in developing only a positive attitude.

Try to redevelop the skills of interaction and communication, cutting out negativity. This I knew was going to be easier said than done. I had being doing things wrong for so long now, I didn't even know about some of them, for example, to relearn how to use a computer again, correctly. I couldn't even double-click on the mouse. These were just some of the wrongs that I would like to rectify.

At Coláiste Íde, I had arranged with the Headway staff to attend in the mornings only. I wanted to see if I could walk, before trying to run.

There would be about a dozen on the programme, some not attending every day. It all seemed strange at first. It didn't feel like being at a collage of further education. More like a group of strangers seeking direction and rejuvenation. At least we all had one thing in common, Acquired Brain Injury. The group ages ranged from early twenties, to a few over sixty. Acquired brain injury can strike anyone at any time.

Just as I was easing myself into going to school again,

fatigue was setting into me. When I got home daily about one o'clock, I had to have a nap for about half an hour. My eyes just didn't want to stay open. This fatigue didn't want to go away. I heard one of the staff commenting on it one day. It's nothing to worry over; it was your body re-adjusting to you using your brain again.

I kept thinking about this new found fatigue, that nobody really wants. So I was musing to myself, there has to be a reason for it, logically speaking, logic being the science of reasoning and all that. A few weeks later I got the answer in the classroom.

The lady with the infectious smile takes a Brain Injury awareness class. Taking the class this day, she gave out these folders that had been made up for the programme. On the front cover was a picture of a human shaved head, with a brain imposed inside the skull. The brain was divided up into five main sections, plus the brain's stem. Each section was in a different colour and was named: the Frontal Lobe, the Parietal Lobe, the Occipital Lobe, the Temporal Lobe, the Cerebellum and the Brain's Stem. Upon opening the first page of the folder, I found it was an imposed brain, pointing out the Frontal Lobe. Then it explained all about the Frontal Lobe and its functions. It controlled nearly everything one needed for daily living, from expressive language, emotional control, the inhibition of impulses, the motor integration and the voluntary movements.

Looking through the folder, it suddenly dawned on me all these things that the brain does. There was also a list of some changes that can occur, because of a person's brain injury. There was the answer to all this fatigue. All of the normal functions, plus the negative ones that I had picked up because of the brain injury, were now in use. The answer was: keep going, but make sure it was controlled usage and not overdoing it. At the same time try and cut out all negativity where possible. After a couple of months, there was no fatigue and I had learned how to pace myself into the bargain.

After going there for a few months, I found it very hard to switch off because of the initial impact of the damage to the brain, so I was hyper-sensitive. I was gaining one way, but getting a reaction that you could do without the other way.

On Tuesday morning, the lady with the infectious smile was excellent, taking charge of the computer class. This I found difficult at first, having been able to work a computer efficiently before the brain injury. I gradually started to get the hang of it, but realized it will take time. Now I found it very trying to relax and concentrate. The only way forward with this, I soon learned, was repetition, repetition and some more repetition.

With trial and error, I began, to inwardly digest most aspects of the instruction in Coláiste Íde. My hyper-active brain worked overtime at times. I was in one of those musing sessions that I was having from time to time. That everybody is only in charge of one brain and that's your own. It had come apparent to me that an awful lot of people were living with other people's plans and ideas, as their way to go on through life, when these other people could never be in charge of that brain. It just struck me as odd; that this could never be conducive in Acquired Brain

Injury repair.

When I was attending the college for about four months, anger was beginning to resurface again for no specific reason at all. Frustration was not far behind, as usual. This was because everything was taking so much time to grasp in the re-education programme. This anger and frustration crack had gone on long enough. I needed to do something about it, like yesterday. Maybe my silent wishes were about to be answered. One of the Headway ladies informed me that we had a new Clinical Psychologist, who would be visiting the collage shortly. I was looking forward to meeting him, telling lady with intellectual eyes so.

The new Clinical Psychologist arrived out in Coláiste Íde, as planned. He was from the Mediterranean with Latin looks, and smile to match. I was introduced to him; after we shook hands, he informed the ladies that he would have a chat with me first. He was very easy to talk to and a great listener. I said,

"I'd like to write but my head is a tangled mess right now."

He then explained that he would have to conduct numerous tests; and then more tests. It was going to take some time, with me coming to see him once a week. He explained that all the tests were necessary for him to get a better determination of me.

Once every week for months, I was seeing him; and I became very interested in the workings of clinical psychology. At the end of all the hours of testing and talking, he informed me that he would have to do an assessment of all the work that we had done together. Two weeks later he informed me that there was no permanent brain damage. Then he said that he could help me. I was very impressed with this person, who was a stranger to me a few short months ago.

Psychology is the study of behaviour. Clinical psychology is the study of people's behaviour following a clinical event, like a stroke. For people who have had a stroke, a clinical psychologist is really interested in two areas: how you are functioning in relation to your thinking (cognitive) skills, for example attention, memory and reasoning, and, then, how you are adjusting to the changes that are significant in your day-to-day, and future, life.

When I met the clinical psychologist for the first time, I didn't have a clue what it was all about. The way I see it after a few months is a cumulative effect of the introductions, then tests and assessment, to see where we advance from here.

When he tells me that he can help me, it tells me that he knows what's out of sorts, and how to go about it. This is done by developing a strategy to rectify or reduce the effect of the problem. The only thing he doesn't tell me is what he has seen to be wrong.

The numerous interviews and psychological tests are meant to provide useful information on the nature of problems one may have after a stroke. (In my case, I should have had all this done over five years ago, if there was an effective health service).

Now these results can be discussed with other members of a team, or in my case it would be the professional staff of Headway in Coláiste Íde, in order to get a better picture of the behaviour one is experiencing of me. Personally, I don't know if this happened in my situation, but at the end of the day it doesn't matter one way or the other. That's the way, the system works, as far as I could see.

Now that I've had an insight into the workings of a clinical psychologist, I've nothing but admiration for him and the rest of Headway's team in the psychology department. Mine never wavered in what he thought would be fruitful in correcting my attitude and behaviour. As I was doing nearly everything wrong for so long, I found it difficult to do it right or put it right. I gradually could see that my man could pinpoint certain things that I was not functioning correctly on. This was very important, because I thought I was doing everything right. With this sort of therapy, you don't see a vast improvement overnight; it takes time and it's a matter of repetition, repetition, repetition, until the message is put into operation.

One of the specific problems with me was that, in conversation, I kept flying off on a tangent. My clinical psychologist finally began to get through, drawing a diagram of a mythical river and by showing me how my conversation kept meandering off course. Eventually the penny dropped. My way, one would have had a far longer river. All these things that one is doing wrong, you don't know that you are doing it, until it is pointed out to you. Then it takes time to rectify it.

Everything that my clinical psychologist had tried to change was for the better. This took place, in the best part of a year. Most of what he had pointed out to me, I was really impressed with. Parts of it did gradually seep in to me, but I still couldn't fathom, with sound foundation, some of it. Some of the changes that I was being taught to alter, with regard to my attitude and behaviour, gradually began to sink in. At least I was stepping into line with my own mind.

Though some of his thinking regarding change, especially related to interaction with people, did not go down well with me and probably never will, I can see the logic in it, but, having had a lot of dealings with all sorts in life, I think my way is more suited to myself. As one professional lady once told me, "humans are hard work."

To alter or change one's complete thinking regarding certain types of people, to me, is showing a sign of real weakness. My attitude to these disconcerting people is now "hello, goodbye," as if letting them know I'm in a hurry. By not getting into serious interaction with them, I can save a lot of unwanted trouble along the path of life.

For a person with Acquired Brain Injury, the least interaction with disconcerting people the better. Life can be difficult enough, like having to learn again, why make it more complicated for oneself? My attitude is, keep it simple and keep it short. I would like to re-iterate, what a neurologist said to me some years ago;

"The only people that really understand acquired brain injury are the person who has been affected by it."

In other words it's hard to beat firsthand experience. While all this was being tossed around my brain, it finally dawned on me: I should refrain from each and every uncomfortable situation.

I was attending Coláiste Íde each morning, while the lady with infectious smile was taking a class about brain injury awareness. She was orating away and I caught her saying "living in the now". I suddenly became wide awake, "living in the now," it brought back an old memory to me. It was an old Chinese man that I had heard using those words a long time ago. He was forever saying that if you wanted to get in touch with your real feelings, you had to be living in the now.

I remarked on this to infectious smile, who was delighted that somebody could identify with what she was saying. Besides getting in touch with your feelings, one can use them in numerous positive ways. Like positive thinking, awareness of what you are doing and where you would like to go. These four words can be used, if your mind is racing. I have found that by uttering them to yourself, it helps slow you down. Once you have inwardly digested the value and usage of "living in the now;" these are a very handy four little words.

XIII

As I've already explained about damaged right limbs acting as a barometer, I have become much more aware of the weather playing an active part in the movement of damaged limbs. This I discovered on a rehabilitation break in Gran Canaria.

The weather was fowl here in Dublin, as it had been for the last couple of weeks. It was lashing rain even when the plane took off. My right limbs were all tightened up because of the constant dirty weather. The next day, all the tightness had gone from my limbs, like it was never there. My right limbs were more flexible; and to walk with no stiffness was beautiful. When I took a step in walking, it felt like there was nothing dragging me back. I knew this not to be totally true, because, in walking, I only had one speed, slow.

Then, while I was more aware of being in a paradise for non-functioning limbs, I took full advantage at trying to build them up and repair them. In my case there is no physical damage to the limbs, it was all neurological. Whatever happened on the afternoon of the tenth of January '99 is a permanent scar inside my brain, that I will never see, only feel.

I had been attending Coláiste Íde for about eight months, when I got a phone call from one of the staff at the stroke clinic in Baggot Street. Would I be willing to take part in a cardiac rehabilitation research programme they were devising? I told the caller of course I would. "We will be in touch and tell you when it's starting." A few weeks later a letter arrived informing me of the starting date of the research programme.

I was over in the stroke clinic, in Baggot Street, at nine o'clock on the appropriate day. There were fifty volunteers in attendance all of whom had suffered a stroke.

Everyone had nothing to eat since the previous evening.

Water was allowed in moderation, because we were having blood taken, for cholesterol check. Each and every one had their blood pressure, heart rate, lung function, weight and body mass index, checked or measured.

When one had been to the vampire section, to donate a blood sample, one could have a health service executive breakfast, if one liked.

Then you were asked to choose a sealed envelope, which determined whether one came twice a week to take part in the exercise programme. I picked a envelope, that awarded me with a twice-a-week trip across the city. All these selections were done at random, but it seemed funny that all the rebel types were coming for the exercise twice a week.

It was a couple of years since I had seen some of those taking part. They had improved greatly from the last time that I had seen them. You would never have thought that some of them were recovering stroke victims at all. The main foundation of recovery is within a stroke victim himself. Positive thinking; and more positive thinking! It has been my own experience that people who couldn't walk, talk, interact and had any independence, now had most of those qualities returned. With me, I also had the added bonus of my awareness being more acute than ever. Since I had learned to relax, there was an all round well being.

I was also still attending Coláiste Íde every morning. I had arranged it with the stroke clinic, to do my twice weekly visits at three o'clock in the afternoon. It was all go; well at least twice a week. Lady of intellectual eyes remarked to me, was I doing too much? Not at all, I thought at first, but towards the finish it was catching up on me. I saw it out until the end. Now it was just to wait for the results.

At the same time, I was seeing the clinical psychologist every week; now I was really beginning to understand where he was coming from. He was putting great emphasis on relaxation with me; he had devised this strategy for me. It worked like this, sitting down, breathe in, and then exhale, saying to myself, "relax." I added classical music for extra soothing of the mind.

It was now October; "intellectual eyes" was right – I had being doing a bit too much. I was completely worn out with everything that I was involved in. Breath in, exhale, relax and the brain just wanted a complete rest. I was aware of just a place, Gran Canaria. It took me a couple of days to make the necessary arrangements. Then it was Las Palmas next stop for two weeks.

The first day it rained for ten hours nonstop, having started at seven o'clock in the morning. An amusing thing occurred during the non-stop rain; sitting on a balcony, I was watching this black cat sheltering. Every ten minutes or so, he got up strolled out without getting wet. Looked up at the heavens and turned back to his original position. This he repeated a number of times over the course of the next few hours. He must have got fed up waiting, because he suddenly made a dart across the courtyard to be with his feline pals. It stopped raining just before six o'clock; and the next time I saw rain was at Dublin airport two weeks later.

I spent each morning after that, breath in, exhale, saying at the same time, "relax." After two weeks of the same during the day, I nearly had developed as much patience as the cat watching the rain. I found it easier to relax properly since that January afternoon, now long gone. One has to get in touch with one's inner self to aid recovery. It was surely working for me.

By this time, I had got well accustomed with where I went in Gran Canaria. It's hard not to fall in love with the place. Personally it has been a great benefit to me, in aiding my recovery, the main factor being the weather of course; but the neurological lift that I've got from here has to be experienced to understand.

I've got to know a number of people who are working in Gran Canaria, there from London, Glasgow and Manchester and from places as far apart as Scandinavia to Tangier. They all have one thing in common; they are in Gran Canaria to escape the rat race of the modern era. It is purely a haven of rehabilitation with me. When you get accustomed to the Island, you can get the feeling that time doesn't matter anymore. All good things must come to an end; goodbye, for now, Gran Canaria.

Dublin is not the best place in the world to come back to in November. The drab weather didn't bother me one little bit. I was on a high after my relaxing break in Gran Canaria, with most of my facilities operating at a better acceptable level. I was telling myself don't get carried away and never forget where I was coming from. Very important also pace myself; never overdo anything that I get involved in. I was also finding out that, if the mind is relaxed and happy, the body will function far better.

Back in Coláiste Íde, it was a return to the classroom of serious fun. I was still seeing the clinical psychologist once a week; his good work was now making a real impression with me. It is one science that can never be rushed; everyone has their own pace for relearning.

Lady Sister took a class every Wednesday morning, all about Healthy Living. It was meant to get the message across to rectify all the impairments that one had picked up since day one of the ABI. There was a great emphasis on sticking to a nutritious diet, plus all the positive benefits that go with one. The good Lady Sister must have spent hours on the internet finding all the deficiencies, associated with food. Nutrient after nutrient was her order of the day as regards food.

I got a copy of the results of the cardiac rehabilitation research, with a certificate of having taken part. My results looked very promising overall, my heart resting rate had gone down from 66 starting, to, in the end, 56. I still had not come to terms with the HSE giving out breakfasts for free.

In the computer class back in the college, I could now double-click on the mouse. All I had done was to change the mouse around so I could use it with the left hand; I adapted to it quite well. The time spent trying to get the impaired right hand to do a simple task, was an education in its self. One had to achieve in a class run by the Lady with the infectious smile. There is an answer for most things; it's just having patience to find it.

Christmas was coming; so to make sure I was not cold and miserable over the festivities. I booked a break in Gran

Canaria; the next couple of weeks awaiting Christmas flashed by.

At Dublin airport, it was surprising the number of people that I knew, that were making their way to warmer climates for the Christmas. The plane took off on time, with most of the passengers starting the party for Christmas right away.

The first day there was Christmas Eve; it didn't feel like that time of the year at all. No last minute rushing about as back home; lovely relaxed atmosphere; plus it was twenty six degrees.

With self-confidence restored, it was great to be alive again. It was the most serene, peaceful Christmas that I could recall. I didn't come across one argument; not a raised voice; it's a place for a relaxing life.

One Dublin family tried to stay for an extra two weeks. The accommodation was no problem; the flights back home was where the snags appeared. Still all good things come to an end, and I headed back to another year; to a new beginning.

January's dirty weather could not dampen my new found, zestful spirit, everything seemed to be in operation. It was the first year in seven that I felt back in charge. I had come a long way from that freezing cold afternoon, seven years ago. On the tenth day of the year, It was tIme for reflection; events just floated through my mind at a lovely calm saunter. The power of the human mind is unbelievable; it can survive damage that one could never imagine, then come back functioning as if nothing had happened. One might have physical imperfections, but one can live with them when the brain is operating effectually.

From the middle of February, the class started gearing up for Acquired Brain Injury awareness week in March. The week is meant to spread the message, through Headway, as to what brain injuries are all about. Lady of intellectual eyes was all on her own, two thirds of the trilogy were off work, under the weather. The lady achieved what she had set out to do and more. It showed me what one can accumulate by going the extra yard, at the same time not overdoing it. Myself; I put together an A4 page of "A Brief Synopsis of a Brain Injury." What I think is important to a person who has never thought or heard of an acquired brain injury before, was the main theme of my paper

Brain Injury awareness week started with Headway's showcase exhibition at the Bank of Ireland Arts Centre in Fosters Place, Dublin 2. The official launch was done by the President of Ireland, who is also the Patron of Headway. It was good to see some of the members of the brain injury correction fellowship, again. All had advanced so much in the last few years, when one knows where they are coming from. Recovery is really in one's own self-confidence and ability to get stuck in, because nobody is or can do it for you. I'm convinced now that the day you start doing things for yourself is the day you move forward on the long journey of recovery. It can be achieved, because I've lived it and seen it happen. Everyone is only in charge of one brain, on this planet.

Returning to the classroom of fun was just that now, whereas not knowing if you are capable or will ever improve was always a hindrance to recovery in the past.

Now I was growing confident with each and every normal-run-of-the-mill tasks. Things that I couldn't or wouldn't even attempt, not so long ago, now I could tackle at ease. One thing that I became aware of is that everything starts with a thought.

While I was seeing the clinical psychologist every week still, I was beginning to form the opinion in my own mind, that there was nothing further that he could do for me. The results of working with the clinical psychologist were evident to me now. I had slowed down all round. It had now become apparent to me that I couldn't achieve normal run-of-the-mill everyday things without slowing down.

A few weeks later, the clinical psychologist said to me: "that's it; you can achieve what you want to do now."

I was a bit taken aback, only temporally; then I could see that it was just a matter of moving forward. He was supplying one of his staff, a psychologist, to aid me on the next stage of advancement.

XIV

How do you write about all this, from the day my brain imploded up to the present time? I deliberated for a few days, weighing up the pros and cons. For starters, I needed an A4 note-book, which I already had. Then I started at January '99, when it all began. I filled in everything I could remember from James Hospital, up to the spring of '06. There was a good consultation of old diaries and medical papers that I had dug up from here or there. Dates or even years that I wasn't sure about, I started making phone calls all over the place. Within two weeks I had a fairly accurate record of events, over the last seven years.

It was very emotional at times going over the rough phases of some of the occurrences. At the same time it was great therapy, reliving when, where, how, it did really happen. By going over everything it was very productive towards rekindling my memory to awaking experiences of reality. Things that I didn't even know about in the first two years, my mind was now finding out for the first time. This was happening when I consulted paper-work, and then made different phone calls. At long last, two and two were equalling four. Where there had been a void in my mind, these gaps were slowly but surely being filled in. I was finding out unbelievable things for the first time, but by now I HAD matured well enough to leave things alone. At times, I was having a bit of a laugh to myself over some of the things that I was coming across, which had occurred. These I had to let go, for my own good.

Then I had the bare bones of events over the last seven years, all it needed now was some flesh. To me this had become now a positive part of integration into living, free of stress and confidence, to have the ability to make my own decisions.

Yes, I had come a long way, from a person in '99 not knowing what was happening, placed in a void without feelings, as if it was completely out of my hands. Now, in the summer of '06, I have all mental facilities available for usage if required. There is permanent disability in my right limbs, but that has been accepted some time ago. One can easily live with that, after the roller coaster journey, that I have encountered over the last seven years. To be holistic again, was reaching a stage of inner contentment. Finally, my self-esteem was now evident again as part of my make-up.

THE FINAL PIECE OF REHABILITATION:

The last week of September 2007, I departed Dublin Airport for two weeks in Gran Canaria. I was worn out and really needed a break. Two days after arriving, I felt rejuvenated. I am convinced the island has mystical qualities of healing.

Within a few days, I was beginning to muse about everything and nothing since that near fatal day on the 10th January 1999. I felt really good and totally relaxed, like I had never experienced before. It was as if a voice was telling me to stay out of my head, and everything will be alright. Never be in a hurry doing anything, and things will work out.

On the fifth day, there beside the apartment swimming pool, I got talking to three young ladies from Sweden. One of them was in a wheelchair and her two colleagues were the carers for her. The wheelchair-bound lady informed me that she was a victim of cerebral palsy. It didn't affect her now like it had done when she was ten years of age. The medical system in Sweden for neurological illness was explained to me. How she was taught to cope and accept her plight. The result was that by the time the young lady was eleven, her entire system was cleansed of anger and other negative traits. That young lady left a lasting impression with me; one had to admire her courage.

The rest of the time there, I was just relaxing and musing

over the last nine years. How one ditches negative and retains positive traits. Every acquired brain injury is unique, and the strategies one adopts that will aide in recovery. I found also that one must have an individual plan that is feasible. All that is left to do is live life and fate will do the rest.

All in all, when everything is said and done about living, one never ceases learning about life. Because life doesn't stop, it carries on regardless.

MY PRINCIPAL GUIDELINES

Here is a list of things I've done to obtain a level of fitness, after events that were beyond my control:

- When I was able to get moving again, I exercised regularly to build the cardiovascular system all over again. I attained a level of fitness after two years and never looked back.
- Diet and nutrition: When I began to learn slowly about living again, I soon got an understanding the importance of a well-balanced diet. I eat plenty of roughage and low-fat nutritional meals, with ample amounts of fruit and vegetables.
- Relaxation and meditation are two other important factors of rehabilitation.
- Yin and Yang: I also got delicately involved in studying and practising it. Thus I realised the studying of it is mind-infinity. But to keep it simple, I did grasp it; the two opposing forces of Chinese religion and philosophy, infinite destiny; the former negative, feminine and dark, the latter positive,

masculine and light. This helped me to understand life in general.
- Independence and confidence; these are two of the traits that I really had to work upon. When I got to understand more about it, it gave me a sense of self-esteem, amongst other things. To find a proper balance of everything, I had to slow down, learn to relax, come out of my head and restore equilibrium.
- Acceptance, I found to be a large feature also. I had to accept that things would never be the same again. Like most things; with brain injury, you have to get re-educated again even to do the simplest of things.
- Another thing that plagued me for a while was non-existent fears. This I eventually mastered. There is nothing to be fearful of. The non-existent fears were all in my own mind. The only thing I could do was be strong about everything.
- I set goals and worked out a practical solution to apply in reaching them. I made the goals obtainable and realistic.

Boland, Bernadette

The Place I would like to call Home

September is that time of the year when Dad can leave home in the city and drive to Roscommon to visit his mother and brother.

The family all share the same house down the country, which is on the grounds of Clonalis House, the home of the O'Connor Dons of Connaught. This house survived all the troubles in Ireland down through the years.

Madam O'Connor, wife of the owner at that time, allowed visitors to see her house in summer-time only – at a small fee. Granny and Madam O'Connor were the best of friends.

My Uncle managed the farm, as his dad did before him, and lived in a family home on the demesne.

The milking parlour was close to the house.

I loved to walk the fields and pick wild flowers: daisies, buttercups and primroses.

Our country home was small; it had an upstairs to it, but you had to climb the ladder. It was an open house for all; the kettle was always on the fire. Anyone who called got a cup of tea and home-made bread.

When my uncle and his men milked the cows, a certain amount of milk was allowed for Granny, who made butter, which was preserved with salt. The butter was made into all shapes and sizes.

The buttermilk went into the making of the bread. My treat was a glass of buttermilk with pieces of butter floating around it.

My duty was to help granny pick young nettles and boil them in the pot. When they were ready, we mixed them with meal and fed them to her family of turkeys.

The hens wandered around the house and garden. They could lay their eggs anywhere indoors or outdoors. What fun! Looking for eggs and finding them in the least likely place!

A section of the garden was for all kinds of vegetables for a good meal. All produce was collected from the garden. A hen was killed, plucked and roasted in a pot by the fire. At the end of the garden all kinds of fruit was growing: apples, pears, gooseberries, blackcurrants, plumbs and strawberries.

Granny's pride and joy, was making apple tarts and homemade bread complimented with butter and jam. For that special treat, Fudge was made.

We all gathered around the open fire. The rosary was recited. Granny always said the Family who pray together, stay together.

Were we poor? I never knew.

Come Friday night, the local musician with a button accordion called, as did neighbours from around. The singsong went on to the early hours of the morning. My mother's party piece was *"A Mother's Love's a Blessing."*

Rebel songs and all Irish songs were sung.

Come Sunday, we all piled into dad's car. We made a few trips to get us all to Mass on time. After mass, it was to meet the cousins. My dad had so many friends to meet: he could chat for an hour.

The local shop close by had everything. I bought the papers. The family were home from Mass in no time at all. The roast beef was ready with baked spuds and vegetables. The leftovers were given to the cats and dogs, also a pet fox or two.

The evening was a gathering at the graves to pray for our ancestors. Later my Dad and uncle had a game of golf next door to the grave-yard.

Come Monday, my cousins walked to school and were gone all day.

I promised my uncle to help him bring in the turf, while he was milking cows. I got out the donkey and cart and hitched the cart to the donkey. Off I went to collect turf, which was a mile away across the fields. On nearing my destination, the wheel went down a hole in the bog-land. After several attempts, and failing to rescue the wheel, I had no choice but to walk back to the house. There was Uncle Mike wondering where the donkey was. I came clean and told the truth about taking the donkey and cart. All hands on deck, the turf was piled on the cart and taken home. The turf was put in a special shed.

Uncle Mike had to go to the Milking parlour for the evening milking. When the milking was completed, the cows were driven out to pasture. The shed had to be cleaned.

In the meantime, I fell into the slurry pit. I hung onto the edge for dear life. Luckily, my cries were heard! To my delight I was hauled out. My lovely new white coat was in a mess. On our return to the house I did not receive a scolding. All were so glad to see me alive.

The cousins had finished their homework. Time for another evening meal! This time, Aunt Agnes and Aunt Annie were present, who were Granny's sisters. Granny was the eldest of 12 children born on a farm in Manorhamilton in County Leitrim.

The night went quickly, with lots of chat and story-telling. The following morning, bright and early, Dad brought his two aunts to the train station. While they were heading back to Dublin, our cousins had gone to school again.

I walked with the men to the market, driving the young lambs, aided by the collie dog. On our arrival we were allotted a pen. Close by were horses, cows and pigs. A special area was made for the auction with seats all around, to view the action.

The auctioneer started the bidding. All went to the highest bidder in lots. Buyers from miles and miles around were present.

When the lambs were sold, it was time to walk home again and be in time for yet another dinner.

Soon it was time to pack the bags and return to Dublin. My country holiday had come to an end.

Boland, Bernadette

My Teenage Years in Old Ballymun

September 1943, the All-Ireland Gaelic Football Final came round again. Mam and Dad were natives of Roscommon. Mam was expecting her first child. They were seated in the back of the Hogan Stand, delighted with the result. Roscommon won. Perhaps I heard everything.

I made my entrance into this world on the 24th March.

This time Roscommon beat Kerry in the Football and Cork beat Dublin in the Hurling Final. Shamrock Rovers beat Shelbourne in the FAI Cup Final. Glenn Miller went missing over the English Channel. It is nice to share the year with Mary Robinson, Nell McCafferty and Vincent Brown.

1947 dawned before I was taken to Croke Park. Once again, Kerry v Roscommon! I was shouting for Kerry and given a Kerry doll to wave. Kerry won. That was the year the final was played in New York. I was brought to every match until coming to an age when I was able to take care of myself and go with my friends, and get into Hill 16. We got the students' rate until we finished in college. The year they made it an all ticket match, made it harder to get tickets.

Living on "the farm," it was wonderful. My earliest recollection: a rejected lamb that was frozen in the snow was brought into the house and laid before the fire. In no time at all she had come to life. Mother quickly made a hot bottle of milk with a spoon of whiskey. My job was to give it to the lamb, which was to be a pet. Her name was Lesley.

When going to Mass in Old Ballymun, the lamb was sure to follow me. Mass in Ballymun was always packed. The farmers for miles around met every Sunday. Fr. Marley was the Parish Priest. The May Procession took place outdoors every year.

Dublin Airport was very small. That time, you could walk up to the plane and meet the Captain, who in turn gave a guided tour of the plane. One by one the farmers were offered a price for their land. Their first reaction was shock and horror: Give Up their Land? At No Price – NEVER! Gradually over a period of years, the land was sold and so Dublin Airport grew from strength to strength.

Living on the farm, there were acres and acres of land all round.

The first land to be sold for houses was to be named Ballymun Avenue. Some of my school friends' parents moved.

My father was well known for shooting and rearing Irish Red Setters. One day, I went for a walk with the dogs and soon was on the list of missing persons. A search party was called – to no avail! Late that night, a young man knocked and handed me over. He recognised the dogs and gave me a cross-bar home from Santry, as the fields stretched that far.

We got a new Parish Priest, called Fr. Grogan. As my Dad's hobby was woodwork, he was politely asked by the said priest to make a crib for St. Pappin's Church. He kindly obliged. When it was completed, the background was painted by the Parish Priest. He was an excellent artlist.

The owners of Geraldstown House gave a field for the use of a fete. It was to be run yearly with all kinds of activity. Charles Haughey, his wife and family always attended. Tommy Wade brought along his show-jumping horse, Dundrum – a very small horse.

More houses were built from Ballymun Avenue up on the left side. Further up, houses on the right led to the farm. I got to know Mary Punch, journalist, and Henry Kelly, T.V. personality, in their young days. I always walked to school and called to collect friends along the way. Quite frequently I met Father Desmond Connell on his walk. We followed his career in the papers. He was elevated to the rank of Cardinal.

On my way from school one day, I decided we needed to improve our Irish. All parents consented. First we had to pass an oral test, which we did. On arrival, we discovered a house for boys and also one for girls. Our daily task was to jot down what we did daily in Irish. During class we had to recite our work. At night a Céilí was in order. On one occasion, taking to my bed feeling sick, some of the boys called to see me and were caught. Their punishment was to kneel in the Church for one hour.

During holidays on the farm, one day I decided to jump from a height. I broke my fall by putting out my hand, which cracked under the weight. My arm was in a sling. However, I soon went back to school; time to do the entrance examination for secondary school. With my hand out of action, I could not do the exam. All I could do was study in class every day.

Going into our class for secondary school, I was summoned by the head teacher who informed me I could not go to secondary school, as there was no exam result to my credit. the solution was to sit the exam and travel from class to class, wherever teacher went. Finally, I passed with honours and joined my friends in Class 1A.

When class was finished, the local boys and girls went for a walk in the Botanic Gardens. A bar in the shape of a semi-circle surrounded the edge of the grass and a sign saying "Keep off the Grass". All was fine until the boys started a fist fight. The majority of the girls disowned them and went home alone. On my way home passing Tolka House, I saw a sign "Men Only."

Fr. Jim Maloney was our new Parish Priest and he had the gift of collecting money. Everyone who donated money weekly had their names called out in Church and the amount was – Professor Drew 1 Pound, and the Farm Hand, one guinea.

One month before my 14th Birthday, February to be precise, Dad read in the local paper that a German plane had gone down carrying the Manchester United team. They nearly all died. On the dead list was Liam Whelan. He was in his early twenties and from Cabra. He was buried in Glasnevin Cemetery. Say a prayer when visiting the graves. Recall the name of Bobby Charlton, who went to hospital. I said a prayer, and in no time at all he was playing again. Matt Busby had to rebuild a great team again from scratch.

Having reached my 14th birthday, summer had dawned. There was a good few months of good weather down on the farm in Glasnevin. My father was Farm Manager. He informed me that a new bunch of lads doing agriculture were to gain practical experience working on the farm.

My friend Ann and I were there to greet them when they came.

Their first task was to mow the meadow; the second day turning the hay in sweltering weather.

Ciarán Bourke was the name of the lad given the command. He was a born leader who had the charm of persuading his work-mates to carry out the necessary duties. On noticing Ann and myself, he requested water for the thirsty men.

We proceeded to the farm-yard and found a brand new bucket and scrubbed it clean. We filled it with water to the brim. It took the pair of us to carry it back to the field.

When all had quenched their thirst, they behaved like children and throwing water from the mugs and drenching one another; we left them, feeling very annoyed.

The following day, the hay was dry and, not bearing a grudge, we joined them again.

Ciarán, as usual, organised team-work and the cocks of hay were done in no time at all. The first bit of work Ciarán did was to reward all by playing his favourite tune on the tin whistle; asked for my opinion, my reply "Not bad". Going home, said he was going to join the lads that very night for an Irish Musical night.

Bright and early next morning, all were ready for action;

time to take in the cocks of hay. Tractor and adjustable trailer were all that was needed. Ciarán did the driving. All he had to do was to reverse into the hay and the trailer at an angle and slide it under the cocks of hay and raise the trailer and bring it back to the hay barn to be left there.

Time for lunch! All went home with the exception of Ciarán, who went to The Slipper for a pint and a sandwich. Immediately after lunch, it was time to fork the hay into the bam and stack it quite high. My privilege was to drive the tractor with Ciarán by my side. His favourite tune was played so often it penetrated my brain.

The hay finished, it was time for the students to resume their studies. Ciarán qualified. He was the only Dublin lad to do so. He never did work at agriculture but got a permanent job playing the tin whistle with the Dubliners; lasted years and years, until he died. We kept in touch over the years. He was a good friend to the end. The lads played his favourite tune at the funeral to a packed church.

July 1958, my father brought an American shooting for the day. He had rented an estate in Wicklow – with farm attached. To show his appreciation, the American family invited us to dinner. The menu was roast beef. Grace was said before and after the meal. The children were dismissed. I soon got to know the three boys. My brother, Michael, was with me. We played games. The older boy showed me around the estate. An hour later, he proposed to me and I accepted. He had no money to buy a ring. It was a secret engagement. He asked what my plans were. I replied I would like to finish school and go to college. He promised to wait for me.

The family were touring the world. He pledged he would write to me on his return to America,. September came quickly and my father received a letter from the parents requesting that I go to America as a maid; also, a letter enclosed addressed to me. They were angry and refused permission to allow me read the letter. Years later, I discovered the only way to get into the USA was as a maid.

Intermediate class was a busy time.

All classes were represented in a cookery competition. I won first prize. I had to go to the Gas Company to receive my reward.

In class once, I told Sr. Canice an excuse, that I had mislaid my Irish translation. She told me to go home and try the "West Wing" of the house.

Sr. Gertrude had us for English. There was time set aside for reading and reciting out loud. Anyone could be called at a moment's notice after the previous speaker.

Some girls in the class had famous relations – Harry Boland, Kevin Barry and Patrick Pearse.

When I finished school, I went to commercial college.

When on holidays from school, I was driven to the sheep-shearing competition. My dad was the judge. On the way home, we called to the Crofton in Carlow. Angela, the Manageress, asked me to stay and help out on summer work. I did all kinds of work from reception to Manageress. I gave the Vicar a guided tour. Joe Dolan and the band stayed the night after playing locally. A night cap with the band was in order. I personally prefer his brother Ben.

I collected my certificates from college – I passed everything. On the notice board was a job advertised. I quickly applied and was called for an interview. Turning up at the appointed time, I was delighted to be asked to start straight away. The job consisted of secretarial work with the *Irish Glass Bottle Company*, and making up the wages for the men in the factory. I made weekly calls to the bank with a cheque and exchanged it for cash. I had a quick coffee in town before my return to the office.

Having played camogie in school, and medals to my credit, I joined Celtic and was accepted on the team. That year we reached the final, which was played in Croke Park on a shortened pitch. We were winners on the day. June of the following year, Bank Holiday, arrived in Waterford to play the local team. I attended the local dance, quickly spotting David Attenborough, who came over and asked me to dance. I was delighted to accept. Before the night was out, he had given me four dances and I was the envy of my playing friends at breakfast the following morning.

That year, on the radio, was a farming programme, presented by Peter Murphy. Quite often my Dad gave a talk on sheep. What a surprise to be taken there to meet the producer on the top floor of Henry Street.

Pauline was the first friend to get married. Feeling sad at the wedding! Quickly realised one does not die of a broken heart. Along with two girl friends, we walked to Glasnevin Lawn Tennis Club, met the boys, became good friends, danced the night away. Some boy always walked us home –

all college boys.

At this stage, I was living in Phibsboro on the corner of Leinster Street. Boland Newsagents was run by my mother. We spent four happy years there. As her children had no interest in the shop, she decided to retire and sell the shop.

The older girl had a Twenty First. All were invited, including the boys. When the boys arrived, they told me they were shocked to find Mary was older. At the end of the night we went our separate ways. The odd occasion, the local girls went to Charleville Lawn Tennis Club. The band was very good; Ronan Collins on the drums and later as D.J.

Boland, Bernadette

Sudden Retirement

> The Irish Glass Bottle Company started in Ringsend in 1871, making black bottles for porter with sand from Dublin Bay and lime and clay from Clontarf. These were mixed with salt rock and soda and melted in a huge tank furnace. It employed a great number of people. However, in 2002 it closed its doors forever and this marked the end of glass bottle making in Ringsend.

I enjoyed my lunch in the Bottle House restaurant, among many workers. We all returned to our desks at 2 pm approx, admiring the beautiful autumn day, with some sunshine.

Our Personnel Officer phoned me to call to her office immediately.

Quickly obliging, knocking on the door; to be ushered in and given a seat; a hearty congratulation was in order, since I had reached 25 years working in the Bottle House. My reward was going to be a gold watch. The PR officer producing 2 gold watches, I was asked to make a choice, being the only Female to get a reward. The presentation was to be made in our Sports and Social Club, Goatstown, and would take place in early December.

The night in question arrived very quickly. Making my entrance to the hall, I spotted Mick, who worked in the Drawing Office; delighted to be able to join him. A four course dinner was in order, followed by the presentation of watches.

The majority were from the factory. Mick was called, followed by myself. Eddie, our Director, gave the watches to all concerned. A second presentation by John, who gave me a bunch of flowers! Photos to capture the memory! Tables re-arranged to seat 12 people at a round table. Mick and I joined Management. The band struck up a tune, everyone happy to dance. Before the night was over, I was called to sing. My choice was *Danny Boy*. I sang for my supper.

Still working in Sales, I realised things were not too good in the Bottle House. Autumn was to come round again. A notice appeared on the board, looking for Voluntary Redundancy. Several workers took up the offer. Finally, I made inquiries myself, and was offered a package one could not refuse.

John kindly gave me a lift home. I made haste to resurrect my electric typewriter. I Typed my registration with tears in my eyes. The following morning handed in my registration, which was accepted in a matter of days.

My final day was to come round in no time at all. After work, all assembled together. I was presented with a video and a bunch of flowers. A speech of acceptance was in order. Quickly obliging and inviting all to Clarkes' pub across the road from the Bank of Ireland, Ringsend. First on the scene, I arranged all drinks to be put on a tab for me. Greeting all one by one, informing them to put the drinks on my tab, and soon the pub was packed. A few went home early and bid me farewell. The remainder chatted the night away. I was like a bee, flittering here and there; spoke to one and all.

When all had gone home, Margaret and I were left behind. Thanked the barman for a great night and asked for the bill. What a shock it was: the total came to 9 pounds!

Being sober, I gave Margaret a lift home. Early next morning was awake at the crack of dawn. I had a fry for breakfast at home, 11 am. Walked to the Maple House Hotel; met Barry, who was the owner and a good friend. He introduced me to Jack and Bernie, proud owners of their own bed and breakfast, living close to Iona Road – on Iona Park.

We were to meet for 1 hour every day; an understanding we would be there. Taking it easy, had my lunch at 12pm.

Evening time: had my choir, Vincent de Paul meeting, Corpus Christi Musical and Dramatic Society.

Maureen Valentine, our musical director for the choir, persuaded me to join the musical society, (some were dying and it needed new members). Delighted to go along and be accepted. A show was put on for 4 nights in a row. This was a yearly event. The Merry Widow went down very well. After the final curtain, we met in the Skylon Hotel for drinks, followed by dinner in the El Corvo Restaurant.

The very next day, I called to Alice, our local TD, and gave a report. I told her I had typed in my registration in the Bottle House and was accepted. Alice asked would I type her letters. I was honoured to do so, having an electric typewriter at home.

I still had plenty of time on my hands. Ringing Premier Castings, and getting an interview, had my photo taken and filled a form about myself; given a number to identify me.

My assignment: get myself to Wicklow for 7 am in the morning. Before starting the day, queue up for breakfast. Then one had to wait around until being called for work. In the meantime, coffee and biscuits were available all day. My turn was to come round quickly; which had to be done over and over again. At 12 pm, queue for lunch. A bus nearby to have your lunch in!

More work in the afternoon. 7 pm, supper was served. The day was completed. Get your pay-slip signed and the hours recorded. Drive back to Dublin; check in with Alice and catch up with the typing in time.

In the meantime, bottles were delivered to the warehouse from Rockware Glass to be sorted in the Warehouse. The people concerned had their Lunch at 12 pm, canteen staff still there. Irish Glass Bottle Company had their name changed to Ardagh. Ringsend was the only bottle factory in Europe to cease making bottles.

Holding onto my shares, I always attended the yearly meeting. Noeleen was in charge of the shares. Soon the shares were transferred to Brussels; also the Annual General Meeting.

I Keep in touch with the girls. Noeleen is the only one still working – for a few more years.

The Irish Glass site was sold for a large sum, the most expensive land in the whole of Ireland. This has been flattened and there are plans to build 3,000 homes on the site, in apartment blocks that will be 16 stories high.

Buckley, William

The Coming of Mary

> Opening pages of William's book *The Dowry*, which tells the story of his mother, Mary Buckley, née Walsh.

The morning of November 14th dawned with the sun shining bright and early. Anyone would think that the country was in for beautiful weather. As the day rolled on, however, the sky began to change, and ominous clouds began to form in the sky. Michael Walsh, who was the proud owner of a sprawling farm in Glounlahan, felt that, although the sun was shining, the day would turn bad. It was time for old man winter to make an appearance. Experience had told him over the years that the middle of November usually meant that winter was just around the corner.

Michael had a competent man working for him whose name was Sandy. They enjoyed an exceptionally close relationship with each other. They were better friends, as boss and servant, than most brothers were. On their way into dinner, they talked about how the sky had changed since morning, and both agreed that it would make a wet and cold night. During dinner, which consisted of bacon, cabbage and potatoes, which was their customary diet, they talked about how the weather would affect the cattle. Eventually, they decided that the cattle should be housed that night – for the first time that winter.

As soon as they finished eating, both men started getting the stalls ready for the cows. The hay, which they had saved during the summer months, would come in handy for feeding the cattle, both now and during the cold winter that lay ahead. As soon as the cowsheds were ready, the cows were driven in from the field below the house. It took some time to get them in, as each cow had to be tied-up for the night. Sandy then milked those that were yielding milk, while Michael sat on the wall and talked.

Besides its normal uses, some of the milk was converted into butter, which was called "Country Butter," and which had a delicious flavour all of its own. All the work was completed early; and it was none too soon, because, long before six o'clock, the rain started to come down. Slowly and softly at first, and one could see that it was going to be a rough night, and that it was time to get in from the rain.

Michael had married over a year previously, and he had found himself a very capable wife. She did all of the work in the house, and, sometimes, when they needed her, she helped on the farm as well.

During the summer she had helped with the hay, and when the men worked late, she often had the cows already milked when they got back after a day's work. However, the winter was at hand now, and there was not much work to be done on the farm, so she spent her time working within the house. This day was no exception. After the dinner, she went about her daily tasks, – cleaning the kitchen, baking the bread, and seeing that everything was completed before the men came in for supper.

The days were very short at that time of the year, and so, around three o'clock, she lit the lamp that hung from the ceiling. This gave her light to see what she was doing.

She felt a little tired in the afternoon, and so she decided to sit down to rest for a while. She could not stay sitting down very long, however, as she became very restless and she did not know the reason. She was not accustomed to take a rest during the day; so she decided to keep on working.

The house was now cleaned and she went to the turf-shed for two buckets of turf. There was no use in asking Sandy to get the turf, as he was sure to pick the wet sods instead of the dry ones. It was she that would have to make the fire the next morning, and it would be very hard with wet turf. Having filled the buckets, she looked around for someone to carry them into the house, but she could see nobody. Hesitantly, she decided to carry them in herself, even though she knew she should not do so.

She filled the big pot with water, as she had done the previous night, and left it by the fireside. One would never know when the water would be needed in a hurry. Supper was served early that night. It consisted of tea, bread, and butter, and as a treat, homemade jam. The butter was homemade also, made by the woman of the house.

After supper, the two men sat down by the warm fire while the woman of the house washed the dishes. As soon as Hannah had the dishes washed, she decided to sit, also, by the fire for a rest.

She, too, had worked hard during the day, and a rest by the warm fire was something that would help her relax. Suddenly, Hannah felt a twinge of pain in her lower back.

She knew that she should not have brought the bucket of turf in from the shed. Tomorrow, she would call her husband or Sandy to bring in the turf.

It was now around nine o'clock, and already the night seemed to be a long one. There was no radio or television in those days to pass the night away. Usually there wasn't even a newspaper in the house to read. The only time there was a newspaper in the house to read was when someone went to town, either to a fair or to the market.

The fire was beginning to get low now, and there was no use putting more turf in the fire, as it would be just as warm in bed. On their way to bed, Sandy was telling Hannah how lucky they were in having a roof over their heads on such a bad night as this. How many people were sleeping out under the heavy rain?

"Poor people", said Hannah, "God help them. I hope they won't get colds and be sick."

It was bad enough to be out in the rain, without also getting sick.

Hannah had made sure that their bed was nice and warm, for, earlier in the evening, she had put a jar of boiling water between the blankets. She knew that her husband liked to have the bed nice and warm before he got into it. She herself did not like to go into a cold bed, especially in the wintertime, and it could be damp.

Sleep came fast to Michael, as he had completed a hard day's work.

Hannah twisted and turned in the bed. She had other things to think about, and she felt a certain amount of discomfort these last couple of weeks. She thought that the baby had dropped in her stomach during the past week, and she had remembered her mother telling her that when that happened, she should send for her. She did not expect the baby to be born for at least a couple of more days. She just hoped that her baby would not be born this very cold and wet night. She would hate to have to ask her husband to go out in such a terrible night as this.

She extinguished the light as she was settling herself in the bed, and felt another twitch of pain in her lower back. She again reminded herself about the two buckets of turf that she had brought in from the turf-shed. She lay down on the bed, and, although she was very restless, she finally went to sleep. Before going to sleep she moved away from her husband, so that she would not disturb his sleep.

She awoke suddenly around two o'clock from pain that was pretty severe now. She sat up in the bed without disturbing Michael. She knew now that the pain was there because it was time for the baby to be born.

She waited for the next pain which came within a couple of minutes. What was she to do? She listened for a while. She could hear the howling of the wind coming down the chimney, and the lashing of the rain against the window-pane. The pains were coming regularly now. Should she tell her husband about them? She decided to wait as long as possible. She wanted to be certain.

Finally, about three o'clock, she woke her husband.

Reaching over to that part of the bed, which he usually occupied, she pushed him with her elbow.

"What? What is wrong? Did you hear something?" said Michael.

"I think that it's time," said Hannah. "Call Sandy and ask him to tackle the horse for you."

He got out of bed, and, with a fierce shout, called Sandy. On the second call, Sandy was at the door asking what the matter was.

"Would you tackle the horse to the sidecar for me, and I will be with you in a couple of minutes!" said Michael.

Without delay, Sandy dressed and was out the door.

"I am sorry that you have to go out on such a night," said Hannah.

"Oh; such things cannot be helped," he replied.

"Please tell Sandy to make the fire and to boil a pot of water and to have the kettle boiling also," said Hannah.

She continued, "Make sure you take your overcoat and hat with you. Take the bag from behind the back door for the nurse to sit on. Please be careful on the road and do not worry about me. I'll be all right."

Within fifteen minutes, Michael was on the road. He took the yard-lamp, which Sandy had used while tackling the horse, so that he could see where he was going. He really liked that bay-mare because he trusted her to be sure of foot on the road. She had taken him to town many times, and she always made her way home while he was fast asleep in the car.

He took it very carefully going down the passage, but as soon as he got to the main road, he gave the horse a touch of the whip to let her know that he was in a hurry. He had to get there in a hurry and be back in time for his Hannah. Hannah was a good woman, and he wanted to make sure that the nurse would be present for the delivery of their child.

The horse responded immediately, and, with a fast gallop, took off. At the same time, he could see that she sensed when the road was safe, for when she came to where the water was deep on the road she slowed down, and then moved out smartly when the road was safe again. It was very dark and the rain was coming down in torrents. The wind was very strong, more like a hurricane than an ordinary storm.

Michael had taken his hat with him to help keep the rainwater from going down inside his shirt, but, try as he might, his back was getting wetter and colder. He was not long on the road when he could feel the cold rainwater drenching his clothes. He must not let the rain bother him now. He was in a hurry. His Hannah was at home, and, as it was her first baby, one never knew when the child would be born. It was five miles to where the mid-wife was living, and in a night like this, it would take longer than usual to travel this distance.

They were just entering the village and making good time

too, when the horse stopped suddenly almost throwing Michael out of the sidecar. The horse had stopped here every time Michael had taken her into town, and as far as the horse knew, this journey was no exception.

Yes, Michael had stopped here every time, either when he went to town or on his way home, to wet his whistle and to meet any old friend that might be there at the time. This occasion would have to be an exception, for the pub was closed at this time of night. In fact, all was quiet. There seemed to be no one awake in the village, and there was nothing to be seen, not even a dog or a cat. With another touch of the whip, the horse was on her way again.

"Hurry horsey, we must not delay." said MichaeL

There was still more miles to go before they would reach the mid-wife's house. "I just hope she is at home," thought Michael.

With the horse still in full gallop, Michael thought that he would rest the horse while he would be waiting for the nurse to get ready. It was just half-past four when Michael pulled the horse to a halt in front of the house. Michael called out loudly up to the window for he wanted to make sure that someone would hear him. Within seconds, the window was opened upstairs.

"Who is there?" called the nurse.

"It is Michael Walsh."

"Very well," said the woman, "I will be with you in a couple of minutes."

Michael was happy that they would have to wait because the horse needed a rest after the long journey. Sure enough, the woman was down in a very short time, saying:

"Come, let us hurry! Who is at home with your wife? Isn't it a terrible night? Were there floods on the road?"

In fact, she asked Michael so many questions that she did not give him time to answer anyone of them, or so Michael thought. He was worried about his wife, and whether he would push the horse to go faster on his return journey.

The nurse told Michael that she was expecting him to call around the middle of the month, and how awkward it was that this should be the night he would require her help. She had brought a bag with her when she came out of the house. Michael did not forget to give her the old bag that he had brought for her so that she would not get wet when she sat on the seat.

"Who is with your wife?" asked the nurse.

"Sandy, the servant boy," answered Michael.

"You mean there is no woman in the house now?" asked the nurse.

"Ah, sure Sandy will do fine," replied Michael. The nurse was a little sceptical about Mrs. Walsh being left at home without a woman to assist her, but there was nothing that could be done now, except to hope and pray that she and the baby would wait for them.

"What a terrible night to have to call for you", said Michael.

"Such things happen," said the nurse.

Michael tried to explain to her why no one was at home with his wife. He did not want to waste time going for another woman and the night being so bad.

Meanwhile, Hannah was at home, trying to stay as cool as possible, hoping that the nurse would be there before the baby. It was her first; and she did not know what to expect. She knew that her delivery was very close, but she had no one to talk to.

"I wish that my mother was here," thought Hannah. "She would know what to do. She would help me if I needed it."

Sandy was downstairs. Hannah could hear him walking about, probably listening to see if there was anything happening. She could not talk to Sandy, even if he were her husband, because childbirth was not discussed with men in those days. If a woman was having a baby, well then, she should just go ahead and get it over with.

The pains were getting worse now, coming every couple of minutes. What was she going to do? She tried to pray, but her pains prevented her.

She looked at the clock on the mantelpiece. It was a quarter to six. Michael should not be long now.

"I hope," said Hannah, "that the floods have not blocked the road".

She began to think. Had she everything ready for the nurse? She had put clean sheets on the bed since her husband had left. She would not like to have the nurse come and find the old ones on. What might she think? She left the old ones close by. The nurse might need them.

She was sure that Sandy had the pot of water boiling, for he had stopped blowing the bellows for some time. He was always a good worker, and she knew that if she really needed help, that she could call on him. In fact, she was sure that he would be handier than her own husband. Hannah looked at the clock again. It was ten minutes to six, only five minutes since she had looked the last time.

Michael kept the horse going as fast as he dared, because she had now travelled almost ten miles, and nearly all that distance without· stopping and nearly in a full gallop all the time.

"I hope she can keep going," said Michael to the nurse. "It has been a long time since I left Hannah. I hope she is all right."

"I hope so," said the nurse.

It was just around six o'clock when Hannah saw a light shining through the window from outside. She knew that it had to be the nurse. She could not hear the noise of the horse's hoofs since the wind was still howling and the rain still pelting against the window pane.

It did not matter now. The nurse was here; and she trusted her. She had heard other women say that the nurse was better at her job than most doctors, and with such a good nurse, who needed doctors? Anyway, doctors were much more expensive and money was very scarce.

When the nurse entered the house she went directly up the stairs, two steps at a time. She found Mrs. Walsh still with the child. She said a soft prayer to herself and told Hannah that she would be with her in a minute. She ran down the stairs and told Michael and Sandy to make sure that there was plenty of boiling water available and to have a pan ready when she called for it.

She was now ready to deliver the baby. She assured Mrs. Walsh that she would be all right and not to worry. Everything would be all over within the hour. But the baby had other ideas. Minutes after the nurse arrived, the baby started to arrive too. Sometime after six o'clock, on the fifteenth of November, nineteen hundred and two, the baby was born, and within seconds of being born, she emitted a feeble cry. "Everything has worked out satisfactorily," said the nurse. "You are the proud mother of a fine healthy girl."

Meanwhile Michael was downstairs saying a quiet prayer that everything would work out fine, when suddenly he heard a cry. He thought that it sounded like a girl's cry, but he was not certain. He had been hoping that his wife would have a boy, who would have been more help on the farm than a girl, but now that it probably was a girl, he was happy about her.

"She will help Mamma," he said to himself, "and that would be nice for Mamma."

That was strange: calling his wife "Mamma," because it was the first time he had called her Mamma. It sounded pleasant and he decided that, there and then, he would call her "Mamma" in the future.

Within a very short time, the nurse appeared at the top of the stairs saying,

"Mr. Walsh, it is a girl."

"Thank God," said Michael. "I think that Mamma would like to call her Mary, and so would I."

Buckley, William

Boarding School

An extract from William's book: *A Fistful of Memories*

At this point, three of my brothers had finished school.

One day, Mammy asked me if I would go to a Christian Brothers school, where her cousin was teaching. She said that I could not stay at home as there was not enough work there for all of the family. Mother told me that she had approached Jimmy and he said that he would go also.

We met the Brother a couple of weeks later. He seemed to be very nice and friendly. He told us about the games that they played at the college. He said that there were over a hundred boys there, all our age. On that day, we met two other boys who would be going to Castletown also. It would be nice to know someone else who would be going with us.

I know that Mammy loved to see us being accepted in the school. I am sure that Daddy was not in favour of two of his children leaving home at the same time. Mother nearly always got her way and off we went.

The summer had been long and beautiful. Mammy had spent much of it preparing our clothes for going away to school.

Each piece of clothing had to be marked with a special number. My number was 79. Mother had been told what clothes we had to have with us and she made sure that we had all of them. It did not bother me about what I needed to pack to take with me. I knew that Mammy would have everything ready.

I really did not look forward to going to school. It was not my cup of tea.

Mammy did not have us do much around the house, or around the farm for that matter, during the last couple of weeks before we left home. In fact she had made sure that we got special food for breakfast in the mornings. She wanted us to be happy and ready to go. Many times during that summer we got an egg for breakfast. That was a special occasion, as we did not get eggs except on Easter morning and maybe Christmas morning.

Our day had come to go to Castletown. I was in no hurry getting up that morning. I thought that I would hide someplace, but knew that Mammy would be very angry with me. I was not keen on leaving home and leaving the rest of my brothers and sisters.

We said our good byes, and we left the house and travelled by horse and trap to Kanturk to meet the train. It would be my first time riding on a train. The train would take us to Banteer and from there to Mallow.

Mammy and Daddy bought our tickets, each of us getting a children's fare. We were under fourteen at the time.

When we entered the train we saw the two boys that we had seen when we met the Brother in Kanturk. At least we knew someone. I was pretty sad having to leave Mammy and Daddy in Kanturk. Mammy was really crying and Daddy was just standing there with his head down. I knew that he would miss me. Both of them waved as the train pulled out of the station. It was a sad day for all of us.

When the train arrived in Banteer, we saw other boys dressed like ourselves getting on the train to go to Mallow. They seemed to be nice and friendly. Some of them were from Kerry and others from Cork.

We had to keep the windows of the train closed because of the smoke from the engine.

The boys were talking about games, especially football. I did not know much about any of the games, and I surely did not know how to play them. We never had a football at home, except maybe when Dan made a football out of hay that we kicked around the yard or the field or wherever we were at the time.

When we arrived in Mallow, we saw many other boys there. We knew that they were going to Castletown also by the way they were dressed.

The train made many stops on the way to Dublin. On one of the stops I used some of my money to buy a bar of chocolate for myself. It was so tasty.

We travelled by train to Mountrath. There we got off the train. All of our cases were taken off the train and placed in a horse and car to take them to Castletown.

There was a Brother there to meet us. He told us that we would have to walk to Castletown. He said that it was only a short walk.

We walked for about an hour to get there. I was not used to walking, and wearing a new pair of shoes made the walking a little difficult. I could not say anything as all of the others seemed to be enjoying the walk. We finally arrived.

We were then shown to our bedrooms. There were about forty boys in our dormitory, one bed side by side with the next one. The older boys were in a bedroom up the next flight of stairs. It was the first time that I had a bed all to myself.

After being shown our rooms, it was time to go and have something to eat, which I recall being a much wanted meal, as all of us who travelled had nothing to eat since early morning. It ended up being only tea time, but later in the evening we had supper, which ended up being more of the same as we had for early tea. When supper was over, the older boys stayed and washed the dishes, while the new boys went back to their yard to play, or just talk to each other and start to make friends.

We were sent to bed early that night, as most of the boys had a long day travelling.

We stayed in the school over the Christmas time. I had never written a letter, so writing home was a new experience for me. One of the Brothers realised that there were many of those present who did not know how to write a letter, so he came in a couple of weeks before Christmas and wrote one in the blackboard. He told us to copy it down so that we were able to write letters now for the first time.

It was a good holiday but I still missed my home and family.

We played many games, mostly card games, like *whist*. The food was good, especially at Christmas dinner.

Before dinner, we were all gathered in the meeting room. There were over one hundred of us there. It was a custom that all of the teaching brothers would assemble for the distribution of letters and parcels that came from our families. Some of the boys got many packages and many Christmas cards from their families.

It was hard being away from my family, especially during the holidays. But what saddened me most, after missing my family of course, was being on the football field and not being able to play. I had never held a hurly in my hand and I could say the same thing about football. In one of my letters home I told Daddy that I would be much happier going back the next year if I was able to play games such as football. He promised that he would have a football at home for us when we came home for our summer holidays.

After the holidays, we received our grades for the examinations we took before the holidays. I did not do well in them, as I did not have the teaching the other boys had in their schools. As time went on though, I learned and studied and soon was able to keep up with the others.

Every now and then, we were given some money from the office to go to the village, which was just outside the walls. There we were able to buy some sweets for ourselves. A couple of weeks before our vacation each boy was told how much money was needed to pay back the money we borrowed during the year so that we could ask our parents to send it to us. We also needed money for the train ticket home. I asked for a little more than I needed, as I wanted to have some for while I was on vacation at home.

I was very excited about going home for the summer. I was looking forward to seeing all of the family again. It had been a long time since we left home, and returning was a pure delight, especially seeing Daddy and Mammy again. I had a nice feeling that we were in for a beautiful summer, especially if there was a football there waiting for us. I knew that Daddy would keep his word!

We were not long home when we were out in the field kicking the football. Our brothers came out in the evening and played ball with us. Soon, the children in the neighbourhood were there to join us. Once the work in the farm was finished for the day and supper was over, it was time for kicking the football. After the first couple of weeks we had enough boys in the field to play a game. Often we played way into the night, as the evenings were very long in the summer. It was great fun.

As the time passed, I could feel myself getting better at playing. The more I played, the more confidence I got. When the Summer was over and I had to go back to Castletown, I knew that I could play with the best of them. I went back with a spring in my step.

I spent three years studying in Castletown, and then one year in the novitiate, mostly studying religion. Mostly they were good years. I enjoyed playing in the football fields.

When not playing football we used to play handball in the sheds. As the years went by, I became pretty good at playing handball. We used to go for walks along the road for exercise if the fields were wet.

Food was pretty scarce at that time.

I remember that one day we were all out for a walk on the side of the road. The roads were very safe during those times. Once in a while, I saw a motor car. It would usually be travelling from Dublin to Shannon, and mostly it would be carrying state ministers travelling overseas.

After one year studying religion, I was going to be sent to England because I was not that good at the *Irish language.* That was the last place I wanted to go. I wanted to go home then, but somehow, I did not have the nerve. I knew that while she missed me, my Mother would not like to have me go home, as there were so many others at home already.

Finally, I told the brothers that I would not go out to a foreign country. The Superior told me that if I didn't go to England, then I would have to go to the Far East. Finally I said no, as I did not want to go there. I was told the only thing left for me to do was to go home. So, I went home and worked in the farm with the other members of the family.

My mother did not like to see me home but there was nothing she could do about it now. I was at home and that was it.

At home, I did what the others were doing.

On Sunday night they went to the dancehall, and so I went with them. One night I was dancing with a nice girl that I went to school with, and that I liked. The dance was an "*excuse me*" dance, where anyone could come and say 'excuse me' and dance with the girl that you were dancing with. Of course while dancing with the girl I liked, someone came over and said 'excuse me,' and started dancing with my partner. After a while, I excused him again. On the next time around the hall, he excused me again. That was all I needed to realise that I did not like this type of dance.

I recall the next morning that I said to my Mother that I would love to go to America. She actually agreed with me and thought it was a great idea as she had two sisters in America and she was sure that one of them would sponsor me.

> Bill went to America, where he served with the NYPD for 20 years, before retiring home to Ireland.

Byrne, Sharon

Sharon's Story

My Dad was an Irishman; his name was Robert David Byrne. He grew up and went to school in Ireland.

My Granddad used to work for the railway lines in Zimbabwe; he went in the 1930's and, when my dad finished his education in Ireland, he followed my Granddad to Zimbabwe.

My Dad was trained as an engineer; and worked in Africa where he met my Mam and got married. My Dad fell in love with Zambia and ended up living there. I have four sisters and we were all born in Zambia.

Our life was simple; we lived in the Countryside; we had no Electricity or television; we had an old-fashioned stove.

We would wake up in the morning and go fishing; or go into the bushes to look for wild mushrooms and fruit.

My Dad was the only man in the house. He worked in a nearby town called Morbles, and he went to work by bike every day.

My mum and Dad divorced when my younger sister was only 7 months old; and we were brought up by a stepmother.

My dad was the favourite in the house. He taught us everything. He used to say "don't wait for anybody; help yourself."

Education was number one in our life. Dad would say to us "once you have your education, nothing will stand in your way."

My dad made sure we all went on to secondary school. We had a lovely life, growing up. It was a quiet country-side, with just the birds, the air, the wind and the trees. When there was a full moon you could play hide and seek at night; otherwise we would sit in telling stories.

My Dad had two places: the farm where he was buried and another place in the town where he worked.

During the summer holiday we would go the farm which was surrounded by villages. There was an old lady who would tell us stories, the kids from the villages would come and we would sit around a big fire and the ladies would tell stories to us.

On the farm, my dad had an orchard with a man called Manguable, which was also close to the Zambezi river where we went fishing and canoeing.

My dad passed away in 1989 from kidney and heart failure. I was at Finchisi secondary school when my dad fell sick; so I had to leave school to nurse him.

After my dad died, the four of us remained on the farm and we ensured the younger sisters continued with their education and went to college. My youngest sister became a nurse, the other sister went into business and the third got married and raised a family – she did not want a career.

As time went on I began to have problems with my sight. I went for a scan and they found I had a tumour behind my eyes; but by the time they had realised this, it had damaged my eyes and I was blind by 2003; and that's when I moved to Ireland and never looked back.

I have met all my Dad's aunties and his only sister and I enjoy my life here very much. I still visit Zambia and my sisters every year.

Carroll, Nora

From Jamestown Road

My name is Nora Carroll. I am 85 years old and was born in Clontarf on 4 January 1932.

I was the eldest of seven children. I had one sister and five brothers, of whom only myself and two brothers are still alive.

I came to live on Jamestown Road in Finglas when I was very young, and grew up there. The house was opposite Buttercrust Bakery. I went to St Brigid's School, which is now known as St. Michael's.

I left school after my Primary level and went to work as a packer in Gateaux Cake Bakery.

I met my husband, John, in 1954 and we got married in 1956.

I went to London, Tottenham, shortly after that, and we lived and worked there for 2 years. We then moved back to Ireland in 1958, where he bought a house on Glasnevin Avenue, which was then called Ballymun Avenue.

I only have one daughter, Ann. I now have two grandchildren and one great-grandson.

I worked all my life in various jobs in Finglas and, also, in Dublin City. At one stage I worked in two jobs, one in the morning and one at night.

I liked to be kept busy, and was always on the go.

I returned to work in Gateaux in the late seventies, and was there until it closed in the early nineties.

I knew everyone in Finglas, as I cycled to work and back every day.

I had a very busy social life, and I went out every night until I was 83 years old. That's when I fell and broke my hip, which meant I could not do that anymore.

I loved mixing with people and had a large circle of friends. I will say that I enjoyed myself.

Christmas, when I was a child, was always a very happy time. I remember that you would only get one present from Santa – maybe a doll, and always some new clothes.

My mother, Alice, was a great cook and baker. We always had a lovely dinner of turkey and ham. She would also make the Christmas cake and pudding.

It was a happy time, growing up in a large family. We always had good fun. My aunts, uncles and cousins would always come to visit us.

My mother was a great hostess and loved entertaining.

Downey, Brian

My Dad

Hello, Teresa. I know it is the weekend, but I want to send my story to you; so I hope you get it on Monday morning when you go in to work. Let me know on Monday if you received it.

This is a story about my father, to whom I was very close. He looked after me since I was a baby. He was always there for me, and he even discovered me being blind.

The hospital didn't know. They sent me home with the all clear. But my father noticed that there was something wrong by my eyes rolling around in my head all the time, and he told my mother.

She couldn't believe it. She said, "How could there be anything wrong with him; he got the all clear from the hospital?"

Well my father said, "There is something wrong! Why are his eyes always rolling around in his head all the time? He must have a sight problem."

So he had to call her over to the cot and have a look.

So he said, "You better bring him back to the hospital."

So they brought me back, and my father explained the situation to them. So they did all the tests then. It was then discovered that I was blind.

So then they brought me to Temple Street hospital. The Rotunda referred me to Temple Street. So I had an operation on my right eye, and the doctor there – Doctor Fitzpatrick – made a bags of it.

She then said they wanted to touch the left eye and my father said no.

"You just told me that the first operation didn't go right, and now you want touch the left eye! No way," he said.

He said, "I will wait until he is old enough to be able to tell me what he can see and what he can't, and then I will seek help. I will not let you go and operate on that other eye."

And she said, "O Mister Downey, you can't stand in the child's way."

And he said, "I am not standing in anyone's way at all." He said, "I don't want you touching that other eye without me or my wife's permission, because if you do I will sue you and this hospital."

So she said, "O please yourself."

So he did wait until I was the age to be able to tell him what I could see and what I couldn't.

He used to buy these sweets, *Quenchers*. They were in a long package and they were all different colours. He used to buy them for me, and I loved them too, and he used to pour them all out on the table and tell me the colours. And then he used to let me see them. He used to ask me what colour is that? And i would get them wrong; but as time went on I started getting them correct. And one evening my father came home from work and he poured them out on the table and I got them all right. He was amazed and he said it to my mother.

And then I went to the *Eye and Ear Hospital,* and a doctor, Doctor Fenton, looked after me and did operations, and all, on my left eye, and now I have a nice little bit of sight in that eye.

So that is one of the stories about my father. The second story is: my father taught me my independence. He took early retirement back in 1983 from work to look after me, and bring me all around Dublin, walking.

He showed me all the streets of Dublin and showed me down along the docks where he once worked too; and showed me all the big ships and the Gasometer down there. That was the main gas station there at the time. It is now all gone and built on now.

My father drove all his life. He drove all machinery, such as fork-lifts, cranes, lorries and all, and he worked in England for eleven years. He worked for *John Lang*, the builder, there, in the 1950's, and for *Serck Radiators* in Birmingham and other places too, and before that he worked in *Merville Dairy* in Finglas for *Craigie's*, and he delivered milk.

He was a helper on the horse and cart from the time he was 14 years of age, and then took over the full round with the lorry when he was 18. So then he was there until he was 21 years of age, and then he went to England, and the rest is history.

But I want to thank my father for all he has done for me when he was on this earth. And I want to say thanks very much, dad, for all you did for me.

He also used to bring me for walks all around Glasnevin Cemetery as a child, visiting all the relations' graves. Also, he showed me all the great men's graves, men who fought in the 1916 Rising, and he really did a great job. He used to read all the inscriptions on the head stones to me and all, Michael Collins and de Valera, and all, and I was very interested in that.

As I said too, he taught me my independence. He used to let me go off on my own over to Cabra to my aunt and that, my mother's sister, that was. And he was thinking about in years to come when he and my mother are gone so I would be able to look after myself.

He taught me very well. So that is my two stories in one.

Yours Sincerely,

Brian.

Doyle, Jack

The Golf Ball and other Adventures

Some people think it is easy to write a story. Most people can do so with ease.

When I saw that a story would have to consist of 1,500 words or more, I thought that was a hard job, but however, I decided to have a go anyway. Lots of things happened to me, so I decided to put several of these events into one story, and that would fulfil the requirements.

The Golf Ball

People are very fond of saying there is something they wish to do before they die. I had often heard the saying; but it was not until I had to spend some time in hospital that I came across the fact in true life.

Shay was a very sick man and was to have an operation soon. In hospital, time lay heavy on our hands. The staff and occupational therapists were very good; but sometimes we looked for a diversion.

We found a putter and a driver in a locker one day: some doctor who gave it all up I suppose. We dug little holes in the lawn, and many an hour was passed, pleasantly, by putting. We had but one ball. This ball was cleaned and put reverently in a drawer each evening, to be taken out next morning, while the patients waited, patiently, for a game.

One evening Shay came out of the ward with the driver in

one hand and our precious ball in the other. Down in the grass he placed the ball, and I watched, in amazement, as he prepared to *swing*. Then wham! The last I saw of our precious ball was a white spot disappearing out of sight in the direction of James Street. The drive was a beauty. It would have done proud for a man off seven. Shay looked at me.

"That was a strange thing to do," I said.

"That was a thing I was always dying to do," was Shay's reply.

Say no more! Shay had his operation next day. The operation was a failure, and he died that night.

As I knelt by his remains next day, in the morgue, I thought of the golf ball and what Shay had said to me the day before.

Ah well, your troubles are over Shay, your ambition fulfilled.

We will have to look for another golf-ball.

May you rest in peace!

Lily Fagan

"The heart of good nature! The heart of the roll!"

Lovely Dublin sayings! But when I came across kindness and love from a young girl, when I was in hospital, it was proven to me that the saying was really true.

To us who were in hospital for a long time with TB (it could be of one or four years duration), the nurses and domestic staff were our friends. The young and the old domestics, as they called themselves, would make friends with some of the patients, and sit and talk with them and listen to their tales of woe and, in general, do their best to cheer us up.

Such a girl was Lily. She became a friend to me. When I wanted a paper, or a little message, she would always get it for me. If I wanted a piece of leather, which I needed for the prayer book which I was covering, or braid for the lampshade I was making, and my visitors were not due until Thursday, Lily was there to oblige.

But she really proved her worth that Christmas, when I had my big operation. I would love to tell you all about the operation, but just to say it nearly was the end of me is enough.

My ribs were taken down to the fifth rib and my lung collapsed. I got fluid in my lung and had to have it drained. Next day, I got more fluid on my lung and once again more drainage, but I was too weak.

When the job was completed, I went into shock. A blood transfusion was required immediately. But there was a snag. The blood kept on clotting. It took from 10 in the morning until 10 at night to get sufficient blood into me to make me survive. By this time, I was nearly joining Shay.

Next evening Lily came to see me. She asked me if there was anything she could do for me.

"I would love a fish and chips from the James Street

Chipper" was my answer.

She winked at me and said "No bother."

The sister came to see how her favourite patient was (her favourite patient was always the one on his way out). When she saw me lying on my back with a fish and chips balanced on my chest, she said,

"Jack, you will be up and out of here in no time."

The sister was right; from the time I ate Lily's fish and chips I began to recover, and never looked back.

Lily, wherever you are, Thank you and God Bless You.

To Rob The Cross

Ag Dul Siar ar m'Aistear!

Maybe the spelling is incorrect, but the thoughts are still the same.

When I was about 10 years old, this was thought to be a school lesson. I thought I would be too young to go back on my memory, and would have to be at least 70 years old to recall my memories; and that would be a whole lot of years away. Now, at the age of 91, I have enough memories to fill about a dozen books.

There is one thing that happened, and I will relate it to you. This story is true.

My Mam and Dad were the best in the world. Both have now gone to Heaven. All our memories of childhood were laughter and joy. Sadness came; but we were all taught to overcome it by trying to be happy despite the odds. This was to stand to our family later in life.

Sometimes things happen to people to put them off religion, and two or three things happened to my mother and father that would have put me off, but not my parents. Some priests think that the church was put there for them, said my mother, but really they were put there for the church.

The brother was a bit of a devil when he was young. He did not do the things he did to get other people into trouble; they were just childish things.

Good Friday; all cleaned, oiled and adjusted. Up to the chapel to kiss the cross. Boots shining. Away we go. Boy, the length of the queue! Long, long faces! Two more go up.

Down on your two knees! Reverently kiss the cross, rub with a piece of cloth; up and make way for the next person.

Mother is busy with her Rosary, and away in thoughts of the sadness of the day and the thoughts of brighter things ahead on Sunday. Mam always said the sun danced on Easter morning at daybreak. We could not prove this as we did not know anyone who got up that early.

Something wrong up ahead!

The line has stopped its slow movement. Mam looks up.

"Do you own that child?" an angry voice asks.

Mam looks over at the far side of the church. There is the five year old little brother proudly marching down the church with the crucifix in his arms.

Mam clears leather.

Bob is caught and frogmarched up to the front. Put it down. He does. People glare. They smile and say "kids will be kids."

But things that happen outside should not happen inside the chapel. Mam scurries out of the chapel in disgrace.

Outside the family gather round, fearful. Mam smiles at us.

"I have heard about the fellow that would rob Jesus off the cross, but Bob took the whole lot."

We all breathe a sigh of relief. Mother is all we worry about. When she can smile, and all the trials and troubles she has, the world, as far as we are concerned, is at peace.

Doyle, Jack

Childhood in the Liberties of Dublin

Life is really funny!

When you think that the powers-that-be are putting a charge on sugar because children are getting too obese, a nice word for fat!

When we were young, there was no fear of the children putting on weight, and I will tell you the reason. Life was free and easy for children as they could roam round the roads without fear of being molested and, as there was very little traffic, play their games on the streets.

For the girls, the main games were skipping and *QUEENIE-I-O, WHO HAS THE BALL*? This was a grand way to keep fit. The boys had a large range of games, including Three-foot Spring, Catchy, Relievio, Football and Cricket. People are going to gyms to do the same things but paying a lot of money to become members of these gym clubs.

When I think of my life-style as a 10 year old (I am just 92) I thought I would try to recall my adventures in the city centre. The area around the district in which I lived was surrounded by factories, farms, racing stables, and even a furrier. All these places were a source of joy to a young lad who was foot-loose and free.

To start, when going to the bakery in Patrick Street, I had a grand lot of ways to get there, from Cork Street out to

Ardee Street.

There was a builder's yard here, and maybe a man would be doing some job of interest, so I lingered there for a time.

Then on down to Mill Street, where O'Keeffe's, the knackers, had a large factory! There could be a poor old horse ready for execution, and I looked on while a man placed a bell-shaped instrument at the head of the horse and tapped it with a hammer. There was a loud bang and the poor horse dropped down dead on the floor. As this was an everyday occurrence, it did not affect my young mind.

On down to the Rabbit Factory, not much to see there, most work was done behind a door! Next to New Row, where Jacobs, the biscuit company, has a saw mill. A man working there was my pal's father so he did not mind if I stood for a while and watched him work.

Round the comer to Dean Street and into Patrick Street! The shops there had a lot of stalls outside; and it was lovely to see the oranges, apples and bananas laid out in lovely rows and a lady watching them like a hawk, just in case someone tried to have something without paying

Now I have at last arrived at Kennedy's Bakery. The fresh bread was delivered each day at 3 o'clock, so we had to form a queue until the bread arrived.

When I finally got my bread, I made my way up to Francis Street. On the way I got a bag of broken rock in a shop for one penny.

In Francis Street, I had to go to Kerns, Butchers. Now

sausages and pudding was the last message.

A short cut through Carmen Hall and into Meath Street and down the hill to the Coombe! The Coombe had a Maternity Hospital with a lot of steps at the entrance on each side. We always loved to race up one side and down the other without being caught.

On to New Market, and another stop at the back of O'Keefe's! Here the men were bagging fertiliser. The smell was just overpowering but, as we lived in the district, we just had to put up with it.

Back then to Cork Street where the blacksmith had his forge. The blacksmith was a very kind man who would allow the children to look at him while he would shoe a horse. Sometimes he would make a horse's shoe, and it was always very thrilling to see him plunge the red-hot shoe in the water and hear the sizzle as the hot steel cooled down.

Now it was a good idea to go home with the messages. Mother knew that I was doing no harm and I always got home at about the same time. I was a bit of a happy wanderer, and going for a message was an adventure to me.

Around Weaver Square there was a convent. The front entrance was used as entrance to the girl's school and around the corner was Brown Street, and this was used for a boy's school. The boys were educated in this school until they were 6 or 7 years old and then they graduated to a school of their parent's choice.

The school, on graduation, used most was the Christian

Brother's School on Donore Avenue. Most of the boys remained in this until they were about 14 years old and some went to work and others to further education.

At the top of Brown Street, Donnelly's, the pig people as we called them, had an entrance to their slaughter-house and the sheep and pigs were brought in through this entrance prior to slaughter. We would all stand around to watch the poor animals being brought in from the big Lorries, kicking and screaming, to their doom. Later the animals would appear as rashers and sausages in lovely cartons in the front of Donnelly's factory in Cork Street.

We had to suffer the smells coming from a lot of factories dotted around the district. Will's tobacco factory, Jacob's biscuit factory, Scribona's cake factory, Guinness' brewery, along with the other factories mentioned already. All these factories gave a lot of employment to the people living in this district, which was also known as the Liberties, so we put up with the stinks.

To go forward a few years in my life, one would have to mention the war years. Now life changed. No longer would one see oranges, apples or bananas. Every item was rationed. People had to have coupons for clothes and bread. All the cars were missing as the petrol was all used for the war effort. Although Ireland remained neutral, a lot of young men went to join the British Army.

The war was felt here in the city, even though we were supposed to be exempt from attack.

One night, my brother and I could hear aeroplanes flying

overhead. This was very unusual. I looked out the window and saw that the search-lights from the barracks around us, One in Griffith Barracks and the other in Portobello Barracks, had a German plane caught in their lights.

My brother asked me what would we do, and I replied, cover your head and go asleep. This we did and slept soundly. My parents and my sisters were all in the kitchen waiting for a bomb to drop. Dad looked in to see how the boys were enjoying the show and saw two boys curled up and sleeping soundly.

Next morning, we found a bomb had landed in the houses on the South Circular Road just up at the top of our road, and had done a lot of damage.

There was a house near Sally's Bridge, and there had been a very big cage in the side window and a lot of exotic birds inside. Now the window was broken, as was the cage, and some of the birds had escaped and others were killed and lay in the end of the cage. This was a sad sight as most children spent many moments admiring the beautiful birds; and now they were all gone. Such a waste, after all the time somebody had spent collecting the birds and now they were gone in one night's destruction!

Bombs also fell on the North Strand an there were a lot of people killed and maimed. One bomb fell in the Phoenix Park, near the Phoenix Cricket Club. All the windows in the pavilion were broken, and a lot of damage done to the building. The match was played as usual on the following Saturday.

I forgot to mention the precautions taken by the Government for the safety of the population. Air-Raid shelters were erected in various places. These consisted of long concrete structures with an entrance at two ends. Seats, etc, were provided for the comfort of the citizens. Where there was a park, the area was excavated and a suitable shelter was built underground.

The Air Raid Precautions organisation (ARP) was formed. Any person, of the right age who wished to help in the safety of others was trained in precautions to be taken in the event of an attack. We also had the Red Cross, the John's Ambulance Brigade and the Knights of Malta, who were skilled in treating wounded citizens.

The Local Defence Force (LDF) was formed, and men and women were trained in armed warfare in case of an invasion. Suitable clothing, boots and oil capes were all provided.

All citizens had to go to certain centres to have a suitable Gas Mask fitted. The Gas Mask, must, by order, be carried at all times by citizens when outdoors.

When the war was over the shelters had to be demolished. This was done by swinging a large steel ball on a chain a number of times against the shelter. The shelter was made of reinforced concrete and their demolition required a lot of work. Large crowds were always to be seen at this free sideshow. The shelters built underground were filled in and suitable trees and plants sown in the ground, and this, when the trees grew, wiped away the memories of the vicious war in which a good lot of good men and women were killed.

It would be hard to write a story without mentioning my Dad, and his love for *Fairy House* and the races there on Easter Monday. Dad loved to go to the races, and had done so every Easter since he was a young man. When the Rising took place in 1916, he was keeping company with my mother. On his way home he stopped at my Grandmother's house to give a bunch of flowers to my Mam. My Grandmother asked him was he mad, as her son, Denny, had just gone out of the house with his gun, to fight for Ireland. Granny was right, Dennis, later my uncle, had gone to Boland's Mills, where an Irish Battalion had set up one of their strongholds. He, like the rest of the garrison, later surrendered and spent many a long day in an English prison.

My Dad was not aware that the Rebellion had taken place.

To go to the Liberties today and see all the changes, to a man as old as me, would amaze you.

Where the apple shop was in Patrick Street was now a big lot of flats. The new name for these is "furnished apartments."

When you went over Dolphins Barn Bridge in my young days, you were in the country. Now you are only starting to greater Dublin. With the new roads and fast cars, the travel just takes half the time.

Even with me, it would have taken me a few days to write out this story, but now I can print it in about two hours. I don't have to go to the printer to have it copied, I just press a button and the job is done in a few minutes.

Doyle, Jack

The Turkey and Ham

"Christmas! Christmas! Humbug!"

So says Scrooge and, if he had lived until today, he would be about 200 years old, and die of a heart attack with the price of his electricity bill. But the *Christmas Carol* had nothing to do with Christmas in our house.

Usually, on Christmas Eve, Dad came home with the turkey. He always left it late, as he said he could get it cheapest at the last minute.

Then, sleeves rolled up, he would proceed to clean the turkey. We would, some of us, stand and look in awe at his skill. Dad would teach us the certain parts to pull out and the parts with which one had to be careful.

This part he called the Craw, and was full of poison. I do not know if he was kidding but, in later life, when I had to do the job, I took no chances.

Meanwhile the making of the Plum Pudding was proceeding elsewhere.

With five girls, ranging from 12 years old to 1, Mam had all the help in the world. Some were mixing; others seeing that all the pots, etc. were gleaming clean, and others in the way.

The pudding made, it was tied in a white cloth and laced reverently, in the big pot.

Having been on the gas stove burner for the agreed time, the cloth was lifted, a long poker threaded through the knot on the top of the cloth. Two chairs were placed, back to back, a big basin placed between them and the pudding balanced by the poker between the chairs. When it was deemed the water was sufficiently drained, we released the prisoner and the girls (aged 12, 10, 8, 2; baby too young).

The steam would dampen all the walls in the kitchen and scullery; and Dad would have a job sticking back wallpaper later.

The thrill of Christmas night for Bobby, my young brother, and myself, was beyond all dreams. When we awoke in the morning, at maybe 5 o'clock, we were awed to see two lots of toys and books with our names printed on one or the other.

We would rush into Mam and Dad, to show them our lovely presents from Santa. They both admired all the loot and placed us back in bed.

As the girls slept in a separate room, a NO GO area, we did not know until the following morning of their presents. We bet, all the same, they were not as good as ours. Dolls and make up! Who wants things like that?

When it was time for the Christmas Dinner, the ritual was almost sacred. Five children, with anxious faces, looked longingly at the turkey. Dad got the knife and sharpener and pretended to be a butcher, and, to our delight, began to carve. Each slice was just as long as the next, so that no one would get any more than their share.

Meanwhile, the ham was getting crisped in front of the fire, no fat wasted in our house, as none of us ever put on excess weight.

Then Dad would do the same trick as he did with the turkey; and we were nearly ready. Potatoes and cabbage and sprouts, prepared long since by Mam and the girls. Plates, knives, and forks were at the ready, while Mam performed her miracle of the Turkey and Ham.

The remains of the turkey were used on St. Stephen's Day and the giblets used as soup, which we all loved. Like savages, some of us would enjoy the different parts, while others would look on with distain.

As we all grew up and things were not so hard to come by, we all longed for the Christmas of long ago. But we should not live in the past. Life-is very good to most of us and, no matter what happens, God is on our side.

Doyle, Jack

The Bus Pass

When it was decided that a Senior Citizen would receive a Bus Pass, we were all so pleased!

At first, the pass could only be used between the hours of ten o'clock in the morning and four thirty in the evening. This was all grand; and then it was found that the pass was no use for an appointment in the hospital at ten o'clock; or to use if delayed in the hospital after four thirty. After much lobbying, it was decided, by the Government, to allow the use of the Pass for all day and night. Enough said.

My wife, who was a little older than me, not a lot, received the Pass and I could travel with her, free. We were very pleased. We now could travel to Galway, Cork, or any place in the twenty-six counties, free. We used our pass to great advantage for some time, until I also got a Bus Pass. When my wife was busy, I would go off into town and view all the sights from the top of the bus.

I would decide if I should go to Rialto or Crumlin, and view all the changes in Dublin since I was a child. At first I would go upstairs and view the buildings as if I was going on a mystery tour, and, after a while, with my wife, would go to Bray and then back to Killiney, just for the ride.

One great memory was the Retired Printers Group. We would assemble at an agreed place and visit places of interest. The Museum, Dublin Castle, Patrick's Cathedral and *Árus an Uactaráin* were all in our travels. One visit was to Carlow and we were brought to the Court House. The chief judge there was the daughter of one of our group, and we were treated well. Tea in the Judge's quarters no less; and a wrap up in case we got hungry on the way home!

This lasted for 20 years; and then my wife got sick and could not travel, and I had to go alone. I still went for a few spins but I found the stairs getting steeper, so I remained downstairs.

I would go to George's Street to the Two Euro Shop, and, having browsed around for some time, get the bus outside back home. On reaching home, the family would ask how much I did spend; and I would reply 18 Euro. They would all say, "Dad has broken the bank again."

My wife died and our travelling together came to an end, and so did 70 years of friendship; but the memories linger on.

After some time, when I got on the bus, I just sat in the front seat, downstairs, as I now found the stairs had grown very steep, and, if the bus was full, I would be grateful if some young person offered me a seat.

This came to an end, as I found walking to the bus stop too far; and my poor old Bus Pass was redundant. I was now stuck in the house unless someone came and brought me to Mass or out for a spin.

But all changed. The District Nurse introduced me to Clareville Day Centre. A bus called to my house and a grand lady helped me to climb aboard. I was welcomed by all the people on *board.* The bus travelled all around districts which were new to me. Cremore Lawn, Tolka Estate, Griffith Drive, Benevin Drive, Glasnevin Oaks, Old Finglas Road, etc. Although I had passed these places before, I was now able to take notice of the houses, as the people got off the bus to go to their respective homes.

On arrival at Clareville, I was introduced to the people, I felt like a new boy at school, and I was made to feel at home. I joined the Art Class and the rest is history.

Thank you Clareville, and all the lovely people, for looking after and watching over each and every one of us!

Engledew, Mary

A Varied Life

Chapter 1: Early LIfe

I was born in Kiladysart, County Clare on the 14th of February, 1923, as part of twins to Vincent and Mary Hehir.

My sister, Patricia, and I were the eldest of six children. I have a brother, James, and sister, Ann, and two other sisters who have now passed away: Joan, and Sheila. My Dad died in the seventies and my mother in the eighties at the ripe old age of ninety six.

My father was a farmer and my mother was a home-maker. We had a large farm with breath-taking views over the Shannon Estuary. We had very happy times on the farm where we kept dairy and beef cattle; also sheep, poultry, and pigs. We lived in a large country house comprising four bedrooms, scullery, and pantry. Our life was hard-working. However we were self-sufficient for food and fuel.

We did not have electricity in those years, nor the conveniences of modern machinery. We used horses for ploughing, drilling, and carting; and we used to travel to mass on a pony and trap.

Chapter 2: School

My sister and I began school on the first of September, 1927. The teacher was my aunt, Lena Quigney Hehir, and there were seven other children in my class. Most walked to school barefoot; however my sister and I were fortunate to have shoes. Unlike today, there were no school uniforms, no pocket money, no school transport – so, therefore, we walked to and from school

My best friend was Bridged McMahon, and she sat beside me throughout national school. I made my Holy Communion in 1932 with Fr O'Donohue, and was confirmed three years later.

Most of the children left for good after national school, to work on the farm or business, while others went to work in shops, or domestic service.

Unfortunately, jobs were scarce, due to the depression of the thirties, and many of my friends later emigrated to England, or America.

My sister and I went to secondary school to Roscrea, in County Tipperary. We stayed in lodgings with Mrs Maher, and our accommodation was frugal. We survived on food parcels, which were sent from home every Friday.

My hobbies were singing and dancing, as there were no televisions in those days. People travelled around on bicycles, and on long journeys they used the train.

At home, we had a wireless and loved to listen to music in the evenings. My favourite singer was Glen Miller, and we also listened to the news, and topics concerning Germany and the World War. We listened to the infamous Mr. Joyce (Lord Haw-Haw) during the war.

Chapter 3: World War 2

World War Two coincided with some of my years in Secondary School; from 1935 to 1942. It was a very difficult time, and food rationing affected us all.

We were glad that Mr De Valera kept Ireland neutral. On leaving school in 1942, I went to St James Hospital in Dublin to train as a nurse. On completion of my training I went to Guys Hospital to train as a midwife. I was accompanied by my sister Patricia, who joined the British Civil Service, and this was at the end of World War Two.

London was a fun place to be. My first job, after qualifying as a midwife, was to work at St Thomas Hospital at London Bridge, where I stayed for four years.

During my term there, I befriended a patient who offered me a job as her personal nurse. This lady came from a wealthy family which had a residence in London and an estate in Scotland. I used to travel with her, look after her, and give her medicine. Unfortunately after four years she became extremely ill and passed away. I was privileged to receive a bequest of one thousand pounds in her will. Her family asked me to stay on as their personal nurse. However, I decided to move back to Holles Street Hospital in Dublin, where I spent two years.

In 1949, I moved to St Kevin's Hospital in Dublin, which is now known as St James', where I spent two years in general nursing.

Chapter 4: My Years In Africa.

In 1955, I moved to Nairobi in Africa, where I spent five years in Maicarbarry Private Hospital. In 1960, I moved to King George the Sixth Hospital in Nairobi, which was known then as the best hospital in Africa. In 1964, I moved to Kalkemega Hospital in a rural part of Kenya on the Ugandan border, where my matron was Miss Costello from Limerick.

We did not get on very well, and I succeeded her as matron in 1968. I remember a very dramatic episode in 1969 where one of the nurses was kidnapped by terrorists, but thankfully she was released unharmed.

I took a year off in 1970, and returned to Ireland, and also went to visit the UK. I returned to Africa in 1971 until 1975, where I worked in a variety of assignments, most interestingly on a hotel-ship operating out of Capetown, South Africa.

Cbapter 5: Marriage

I spent in total about twenty years in Africa, and really enjoyed the expatriate way of life. I met some great friends, whom I am still in touch with to this present day.

During some social gatherings, I met my future husband, Jimmy Engledew. Jimmy was a big-game hunter who was on safari in the jungle and bush of Kenya and Uganda for up to twenty years. In 1971, for our engagement, we went by private plane to Mauritius, and later we got married.

I always recall the remark made by the priest at our wedding day that he preferred funerals to weddings, as they were more permanent.

Jimmy was a fantastic cook and his barbecues were always a treat.

Chapter 6: Our Return To Our New Homeland

In 1975, Jimmy and I returned to Jimmy's home town of Dawlish on the South Devon Coast of England. We were residing just ten miles from Exeter Airport. We purchased a large house which we named after the largest mountain in Africa, Kilimanjaro.

I began work in Dawlish local hospital, while Jimmy ran his B&B Business. In 1983 I retired from nursing and helped Jimmy in the business. We had a great social life in Dawlish and went to quizzes, musicals, and of course played our favourite game of Bridge. We were members of the British Legion and the RAFA club. Jimmy also enjoyed bowling.

Dawlish is a beautiful town, similar in many respects to Lahinch, only much larger.

Unfortunately, Jimmy became ill and passed away in 1998. We had sold our house, Kilimanjaro, in 1996, and moved to our other house in 2001. I decided to sell this house and move back to Dublin, where I would be close to my family. I live a very comfortable life now in retirement there.

Chapter 7: Conclusion

I have led a very interesting and varied life, from a farm in West Clare to hospitals in Dublin, London and Africa, from where Jimmy and I returned to Devon after marriage, and then my retirement in Dublin.

I have witnessed many changes in my lifetime and am blessed with good health and am now enjoying my retirement in Dublin.

Ingoldsby, Seán

Highlights and Not-So-Highlights of a Young Life

The Tommies

One of my very earliest memories, and vague enough, was at five years old.

I was with my father on the Clontarf Road, and we sighted, as we often did later, a passenger-steamer moving down the Liffey past the docks, and we could hear, wafting across the water, the cheering and singing of the occupants.

My father told me that this was the "British Tommies" going home.

Needless to remark, that made little impact on me at the time, and it was only much later that I began to realise the historic nature of this event of 1922.

Boat-racing at Clontarf

A lot of water has passed down the Liffey in the meantime, and a fair amount of the same substance has been permanently excluded by successive reclamation projects from areas of Dublin Bay, to which in former times it had free access.

For example (and it is not the only example), the thriving industrial area on the north side of the East Wall Road was, in my younger days, the open sea, and, in fact, there was a small, but thriving, sailing club headquartered opposite the pub then called the Wharf Tavern (now Seabank House); and many a thrilling yacht race I witnessed there, around a course which brought the boats first over towards Clontarf Road, then out parallel to a mark near the then thriving Clontarf Baths, with a long reach back home thereafter.

Most of the dozen or so boats were old enough for that time (late 1920s to mid-1930s), but there were two extremely racy boats, identical twins, modelled on a type popular in Sydney Harbour, Australia, and named appropriately *Parramatta* and *Malabar* (after two suburbs of Sydney). They had been built in Ringsend by the best-known boat-builder in Ireland at the time, one Sonny Kearney. Their masts and sails were half as tall again as the length of the boat, and, as they were extremely fast, they were normally handicapped to give many minutes' advantage to their slower fellow competitors and usually succeeded in beating them all nonetheless.

My Model Yacht

As will, I'm sure, be apparent from the foregoing, I was keen at that time on anything to do with yachting, and nautical matters generally. So much so, that my Dad was kind enough, not to mention competent enough, to make for me a model yacht, roughly two foot six from stem to stem, Tall-masted and complete with mainsail, foresail, close-reefs, a lead hull, and with its plywood deck accurately painted as slats to represent planked decking.

We used to cycle to the Dollymount tram terminus, and Dad, having adjusted the sails to suit the prevailing west wind, would launch the yacht to sail to the Bull Island across what is now the well-known bird sanctuary, but at that time more usually termed the *Blue Lagoon*.

One unhappy day, however, we made insufficient allowance for a rapidly ebbing tide, with the result that my precious craft, instead of grounding on the sands near the Sea Scouts' den, as programmed, was carried on the ebb tide under the wooden Bailey bridge, out of the reach of vainly clutching hands. Thereafter, she continued the south-westerly course in the general direction of the Pigeon House, and was soon lost to sight.

> This story had a happy ending. Sean's Dad wrote a letter to the fledgling radio station "2RN" describing the loss of the model-yacht and how pleased his little boy would be to get it back. I think he even offered a reward of half a crown, but I could be wrong. Anyway, a listener in Ringsend had found the boat and was delighted to return it to its owner. Unfortunately, after getting such a fright on that day, they never sailed the little yacht again, and it remained in the garden shed.

Growing up in Fairview

I was born in Windsor Avenue, Fairview, in 1917.

At that time Fairview could fairly be described as little more than a village on the outskirts of Dublin City. The *Marino* and *Croydon Park* estates were what would today probably be called greenfield sites, although a fair amount of the land of Marino had been converted into allotments ("plots" the people used to call them}. This helped to keep the locals in fresh vegetables

The First World War was raging, and many things were scarce, though I, at that stage, was, of course, too young to notice.

The Easter Rising was less than a year before my birth, and I was named "Sean" after Sean Mac Diarmada, one of the executed leaders, who had been a friend of my father's. However, none of this had any impact on me.

During my early years, the main road through Fairview and on to Clontarf and Dollymount was quite a narrow thoroughfare, sufficient only to carry a double line of tram-tracks with a margin at each side, and was just wide enough to take the traps, cabs, carriages, farm carts, lorries and the odd motor car. Buses came later.

Annesley Bridge, over the River Tolka, was humpbacked and extremely narrow, and it would be a brave cyclist who would tackle it neck and neck with a tramcar.

Reclamation of the Slob-lands

The road was bounded on its eastern side by the original sea wall, and the area between the wall and the Dublin-Belfast railway was the "Slob-lands," which were then, and for many years after, in process of reclamation from the sea. In fact, but one generation before my birth it had been navigable by small boats when the tide was in.

My father recalled an embarrassing experience when he, having reported his older brother Joe to be too ill to attend school (in St Joseph's CBS), had been called to the window by the teacher to witness and explain why Joe was, at that precise moment, paddling his canoe past the school.

The task of reclaiming the slob-lands area, and its subsequent transformation into the present-day Fairview Park, was undertaken by Dublin Corporation (in recent times renamed, - doubtless for some good reason, "Dublin City Council"). The filling material used for this purpose was none other than the contents of the city's dust-bins.

During the period in question, i.e. the 1920s and early 1930s, the methods employed were very much less refined than what is the norm nowadays. No attempt was made to cover the dumped waste material with topsoil until it had well bedded down. Needless to say, Fairview during those years, most particularly in high summer, was pervaded by a most disagreeable odour.

The River Tolka, at low tide, also contributed its share to the local aroma, and the best efforts of the Irish Sea to provide the denizens of Fairview with healthy ozone-laden sea breezes were stopped in their tracks as they reached the railway line, which at that time divided the area from Dublin Bay.

People in those times were extraordinarily passive and accepted the conditions without complaint. Lobby groups and militant residents' associations were much later developments.

The former slob-lands area is now *Fairview Park*.

The old sea-wall was still there in my time, and, as a small boy, I often sat on it watching the cabs, outside cars, trams, and occasional motor cars, returning from Baldoyle Races, Dollymount Strand, Howth, Malahide, etc.

There were woods, allotments, and two large houses, where the Corporation later built the Marino and Croydon Park housing estates. One of these houses had originally been the Country House of Lord Charlemont (head of Grattan's Volunteers).

All of the Howth trams, and many of the others, were open-topped with wooden, slatted seats on top. The seat-backs were reversible, so one could always face forward whether the tram was coming or going.

I used to be fascinated watching the trolley as it hissed along on the overhead wires, sometimes coming off in a shower of greenish sparks, on which occasions the conductor would have to jump out, pull the plunging trolley to the wires, while the following traffic (if any) waited patiently behind.

My Favourite Tram Journey

My favourite tram journey was on the top of Number 23.

Ballybough – Parkgate Street

So read the board on the left side, and

Parkgate Street – Ballybough

the board on the right.

This was the greatest pennyworth imaginable.

Under the loop-line bridge; up and over the Royal-Canal cum-Midland-Great-Western-Railway bridge; a fleeting glimpse of Croke park on the right; chance of seeing a train or horse-drawn canal boat en passant; past the Old Maids' Home on Portland Row, and on through Summerhill, a narrow street of former Georgian mansions, by then reduced to tenements.

You'd see old ladies in shawls viewing the passing scene from the iron balconies of upper storey windows, or emerging from the little basement-level yard, known for some reason as "the area," to see what was going on in the street.

There was always something going on: pedlars shouting their wares, groups of urchins, mostly bare-footed, dashing dangerously across the road, an occasional fight, with much vocal encouragement not only from the ringsiders, but also from the grandstanders in the balconies.

Halfway along Summerhill, our parents invariably pointed out to us the house where bad boys were sent, identified later as the *Summerhill Detention Centre*. This was later transferred to *Marlboro House*, Glasnevin, since replaced by the new Meteorological Office. Juvenile delinquency had not been invented then, and the number of boys detained at any one time in the city, (pending, in many cases, transfer to Artane industrial school) would hardly have exceeded 12.

Emerging from Summerhill, on to Parnell Street, the tramline veered left around the Parnell Monument and across the top of O'Connell Street, with lots of trams, Nelson Pillar, the GPO, and, in the distance, the O'Connell Monument, all to be absorbed and appreciated before vanishing from sight.

One hardly noticed the Rotunda round room and hospital on the right, as the tram rumbled on towards Capel Street.

A fascinating glimpse was all one got of Moore Street. As the tram neared Capel Street corner, Just beyond *Williams and Woods* jam factory, the street narrowed considerably, and the tram-track became single line.

Before navigating the narrows, our tram would have to wait until its opposite number, headed towards Ballybough, would have cleared the single-line section.

Left-handed angle into Capel Street, where there were a couple of pawnshops whose signs of three brass balls were always watched for and commented on, also a huge golden key hanging over Smith's Locksmith shop.

Halfway down Capel Street, if you were quick, you could get another glimpse of Nelson's Pillar from the Mary Street intersection, while straight ahead was Capel Street (Grattan) Bridge and the River Liffey, and, in the middle distance, the City HalL

At the river, the Number 23 turned sharp right along the north quays. One could at once "smell the sea," or so we thought, and there were always plenty of seagulls swimming on, or flying over, the water.

If the tide was in, we could be lucky enough to see several Guinness barges plying up and down, laden with barrels. These were regular little steamers, and, as they came to each bridge, two of the crewmen stood by to tip the smoke stack into a horizontal position so that the boat could negotiate under each arch without disaster.

Trams ran also along the South quays in those days (at one time the Number 22 was *Kingsbridge – Rathmines*), and our sporting instincts were employed in speculating that our tram would race and beat the tram on the opposite side of the river.

If our heads could be persuaded to turn away from such a race, you could see the Four Courts, newly restored, and, beside it, the Fours Courts' Hotel.

On the South side, at the corner of Wine-tavern Street and the quays, was the "Irish House," a pub of outstanding design, a facade of round towers, wolfhounds, and colleens (some of these figures are now in the Guinness museum), and beyond that, at the top of Winetavern Street, Christ Church Cathedral.

Below Guinness's Brewery, on the south side, was the wooden wharf where the barges were loaded, the barrels being brought from the brewery proper by miniature trains, hauled by miniature engines on miniature tracks. There was also a full-sized railway heading into Guinness from Kingsbridge (now Heuston) Station, and, on a really lucky day, we might see action on that also.

If we looked to the right, however, we might see the soldiers of Collins Barracks and the river, and just beyond that, an array of cannons and pyramids of cannon balls on the triangular plot known as the Croppies Acre. These relics of the Crimean war are no longer there. Some, I think, are now in Arbour Hill.

By now we could see the Park Gates straight ahead and,

over the trees, the Wellington Monument.

On alighting from the tram, we would watch the driver changing ends, reversing the seats as he passed along, and the conductor swinging the trolley around, and reconnecting it to the appropriate wire for the return journey.

Then we would face into the Park, eager for an afternoon of further delights, including a walk though the People's Gardens en route to the Polo Grounds, and, at the end of the polo match, a spell of cricket at the Cricket Grounds, followed, maybe, if the cricket wasn't very exciting, by a visit to the dog pond – a well-named stretch of water where there was always plenty of action, involving spaniels, terriers, assorted mongrels, their owners, and much pitching and un-pitching of sticks.

It was always hard to tear us away from the pleasures of the park, but, as we trudged back down the main road, past the magnificent Gough equestrian statue, we consoled ourselves with thoughts of the further delights, predictable or otherwise, awaiting us on the return journey, *Parkgate Street - Ballybough* .

Keyes, Pauline

Never Say Die

The story of my life: where do I start?

I was born and reared in the country. I was brought up on a farm in County Laois. I had four sisters and one brother. Life was wonderful.

Mum and Dad were always jolly. Mum was always smiling and Dad was a bit serious. Of course, there were the little arguments too.

It was great living in big open fields with cattle, horses, pigs and plenty of cows. We all had to do our bit after school finished in the evenings.

I went to a National School with very few children attending. In 5th class there was one other girl with me. This was the same in 6th class. Leaving school was sad; there were no more skipping across the fields and robbing orchards.

After that I went to technical school.

At 16, I went to Surrey and got a dental job. I did not like England. I returned home at 18.

I got Polio then; and thought it was the end of the world. The Doctors told me I would not walk again, but I proved them wrong! I spent three years in Cork Street Fever Hospital with open fires on the hearth. Logs were mostly burnt. There was a strict matron in charge.

In 1955, we were the first patients in Cherry Orchard Hospital. I spent most nights sleeping on the veranda. That summer we got sunburnt on St. Patrick's Day!

Moving out to the Cedars, Dun Laoghaire, we were lucky to be trained for a job. We did typing, shorthand and book-keeping. Thankfully we passed our exams.

Anything to do with cash I liked; so I firstly joined Jury's Hotel, College Green. There were lots of staff there.

Film stars such as Gregory Peck, Pat Boone and the Rolling Stones stayed there. I met lots of VIPs. Matt Busby was a frequent visitor, which was the high-light with all the men folk that were into football.

I spent 11 years working there doing cashier work. I moved on to the Russell.

Incidentally, while working at the Russell, I also had the pleasure of meeting many famous people, film stars and TDs too.

Charles Haughey was a regular; he sat in a corner, reading his newspaper. We, also, saw a lot of Tony O'Reilly.

The best of all was when President Nixon came to Ireland in 1969. I had the pleasure of making up his bill, which took place in Russell Hotel, but the Ivy House did the catering. I did not see him; but who cares? He was only another American President.

I didn't mind doing cash work, which was interesting. This would be another chapter in my life.

I retired in 1988, grateful I had such a busy life. I now live on my own and attend Clareville Day Centre.

Bored? Never heard of it!

Slán.

Pauline Keyes

Killeen, Krunchie

Big Boys' School

I was eight and a half years' old when, in September 1951, I started in Big Boys' School, the senior-boys' section of St Peter's National School, Phibsborough.

If you were a stranger visiting the Big Boys' School, you would have a hard time finding it. Yes, you would see the imposing Victorian, yellow-and-red-brick building, but neither of the two visible entrances would lead you to the Boys' School.

Saint Peter's School, Phibsborough

The entrance you can barely see in this picture, on the extreme left end of the building, led to the Infant School. The one on the far end led to the Big Girls School. Should you enter by either of these doors, you would be unable to access the Big Boys' School, for you would find that the internal door to the Big Boys' Stairs would be locked. It was only opened for special purposes, for example to allow Mrs

Walsh and her assistants to bring milk and sandwiches from the kitchen to the Boys' School.

The Boys' School occupied the entire upper floor of both wings of the school: the main, north-south, wing, visible in the picture above, and the hidden, east-west, wing, behind the main building.

In my day, to enter the Boys' School, you had to pass through a scary narrow lane, between the school building and the adjoining row of houses. Actually, boys liked lanes, preferring them to roads.

Laneway leading to Boys' Entrance

The lane (now closed off by a gate) led to the rear of the building, where you would find a back-yard-style wooden door leading to the Big Boys' schoolyard, a rather cramped area when full of four hundred or more pupils – but more spacious than the narrow girls' yard in front of the building, i.e., between the building and the railings in the above pictures.

In those days parents did not bring the children to school: they made their own way, on foot. When we were discharged from school, after classes, I usually made my way home by laneway rather than by Road, specifically by a lane that lay in between Norfolk Road and Cabra Park.

Norfolk Lane

This lane led from St Peter's Road (where the school was sited) to the Keyhole (or cul-de-sac) at the top of Norfolk Road, where I lived. It was also a "short-cut" for kids going to Cabra, because there was a pedestrian exit from the Keyhole to Connaught Parade and, from there, one could pass over the railway bridge on Connaught Street, on to Cabra. (When we said "short-cut" we did not necessarily mean a shorter route, but a more adventurous route).

Near the top of this lane, in fact the last doorway on the left hand side, you would pass the customers' entrance to the Turf Depot, run by Dublin Corporation, a fascinating world much frequented by me and the other boys of the Keyhole, as "helpers," not entirely with parental approval, during those magic years between the ages of eight and twelve.

There, turf (peat) was issued (in exchange for vouchers) to rough entrepreneurs with prams or more ample wooden hand-carts, for delivery to Social Welfare recipients. A few years after this, the whole enterprise would collapse when a Social Welfare Inspector, hearing of their little enterprise, would stop the unemployment-benefit of these rough entrepreneurs. This clamp-down (along with changing times) made the whole turf-depot uneconomical, for turf-delivery was never going to be a viable enterprise in itself, just a supplement on the dole. The depot was soon closed and replaced by a scheme where fuel-vouchers could be redeemed at any retail outlet. This episode would be another clear warning to the unemployed of Phibsborough and Cabra never to attempt to earn money. However, back in 1951, when I was starting in Big Boys' School, the turf-depot was in full swing, and this world was only opening up to me.

At the top of this same lane, coming home from school one day, I found a pile of clothes, dumped. As I approached the pile, it became apparent that they were my clothes, and those of my siblings. Questioning my mother, I discovered that a "poor" woman had come to our door asking for clothes for her raggy children. So, mammy had gone to the hot press and taken a selection of our things and given them to her. None of our things was good enough for the woman, however, and so she dumped the lot in the lane. The woman was not really collecting clothes for her own family. She was one of the many professional beggars who scoured the area, and was only interested in clothes that were good enough to be re-sold on the second-hand-clothes market.

Proceeding up this lane another day, after school, with a group of Cabra kids, one lad burst into a tirade of intemperate language, attacking the "rich" people of Norfolk Road who owned their own houses. (Norfolk Road houses, modest as they were, were privately owned, but most of Cabra was public housing). Years later, I put the sentiment into verse:

> O, comrades, listen to what I say:
> I've got a message for you today:
> Ireland will never be truly free,
> 'Til we eliminate the bourgeoisie.

I was usually very quick to express my opinion, but on this occasion I stayed mum. It did not occur to my outspoken friend that one of his raggy mates was a "rich" kid. The irony was that this fellow always had money in his pocket for sweets, whereas my "rich" pockets were always empty. My parents had to feed a family of five (and ultimately eight) children on a rather small, police-man's, wage. After income tax, mortgage repayments, house-rates, and ground rent, there was barely enough to put food on the table. In those days, Income Tax on ordinary workers was burdensome because Agricultural Exports, our leading industry, were subsidised. Rates on houses were burdensome, because the entire Health Service was funded from Rates. The ground rent on the Keyhole houses, built in the 1930s, was £20 per annum, much larger than ground rent on older houses in the city.

This Cabra kid's parents were on differential rent, which means they only paid the amount of rent they could afford; they had no mortgage to pay, received free fuel from the Turf Depot, had house-repairs done for them by the Corporation, and had free medical service, and so were probably better off in terms of airgead-sa-phóca.

Lack of free medical service impacted on me. At the time I started Big Boys' School, I was suffering from chronic rhinitis (runny and blocked nose), which affected me at least as long as there was an R in the month (and bouts of hay fever when there was not). My parents could not afford to be running to the doctor every week for minor complaints like that.

A short time before starting Big Boys' School, trying to clear a blocked nose, I had burst a blood vessel, giving me a nose-bleed. Mother told me that in future I should not blow to clear my nose, but, instead, hold my breath. This actually worked like magic. Hold your breath for thirty seconds (or heart-beats) and a blocked nose will clear. Repeat for an even clearer nose. The scientific explanation is that Carbon Dioxide, generally regarded as the waste product of breathing, is actually needed by the body; but when a person hyperventilates (i.e., breathes too fast), his store of Carbon Dioxide is depleted, causing the nostrils to clog up. Holding one's breath builds up the Carbon Dioxide and frees the nose!

Perhaps I got into the habit of hyperventilating from being in the middle position in bed, between my two brothers. No doubt, in this position, I would hyperventilate as a means of keeping cool, like a panting dog. There were three bedrooms in our house. My parents and two sisters were in one, my two brothers and I in another and a lodger in the third. Keeping a lodger was necessary to help pay the mortgage.

Another famous laneway adjoining St Peter's School, – down beside the Girls' entrance, gave access to the seating area of Dalymount Park, home ground of Bohemians Football Club. It also led to Neville's Shop, which Mrs Neville had opened at the bottom of her back garden, where we did a lot of our grocery shopping.

One day, when mammy was shopping in Neville's, she found she was served by Doctor Neville, (relieving his brother, Paddy, who usually served). When he asked about the family, mother mentioned my runny nose. Doctor Neville suggested she give me the cream off the top of the milk. Mother tried this; and it worked. However, when my siblings protested, we reverted to egalitarian sharing of the cream, and my rhinitis returned. Eventually, mother took me to the GP, Doctor Brown, who put me on Scott's Emulsion to clear the condition, and Cod Liver Oil for maintenance. This regime worked, and from then on the entire Killeen family was on Cod Liver Oil.

My rhinitis was nothing compared to the chronic condition of some of the children in the school, who had constant "greeners," hanging from their nostrils. Since butter was expensive, many of the families used margarine instead. Their diet was sorely lacking in Vitamins, and they suffered the consequences, in health and in school-work. Butter and cod liver oil contributed to the Killeens' good school performance.

There were to be fifty four boys in my class, and most of them were in good, robust, rhinitis-free, health.

There was an hour's break for lunch, which we called dinner, in the middle of the day, i.e., between 1 pm and 2 pm. For me, home was a five-minute walk from school. Since there was a mother in every home in those days, dinner was on the table as we arrived home. We were in plenty of time to listen to *"The Kennedys of Castleross,"* a radio soap-opera that was broadcast at 1.15 pm on two of the five week-days. After this, we stayed quiet during the News at 1.30, and then headed back to the school.

One day, a lot of my class-mates arrived very early back after dinner. We decided to go up to Cabra Park (a housing estate near the school) to play a game of Cowboys and Indians, and thought we would have plenty of time. The Cavalry searched for the Indians around the lanes of Cabra Park, and, eventually, the two forces came face to face. The idea was that there would then be a mill between the two forces, but, in actuality, there was a stand-off. Then it was decided to resolve the matter by single combat. As the minutes ticked by, back in the school, teacher, Mossy O'Connor, was facing a half-empty classroom with some concern. When the entire cavalry and tribe of Indians marched in, all received a suitable caning.

Krunchie's Class (Confirmation photo)

I once knew the names of everyone in the class, of course, but now, when I peruse this photo of the class in our Confirmation suits, I can identify just about a dozen; and some of those only tentatively.

Confirmation was the Sacrament that made us strong and perfect Christians. Of course, it only worked if one put it into action. It was no longer sufficient to avoid stealing, lying and violence; you also had to manifest these good qualities to others. So, when offered a fruit of the "Free Counter" in the school yard, instead of just saying "No thanks," being now a soldier of Christ, I went on to explain that I did not consider it proper to receive stolen goods. I was overheard by a streetwise classmate who exclaimed, "Hey, Killeen, you actually believe all that stuff!" He called a few buddies over, and then, with this selected audience, taunted me about professing to be an upright citizen and Christian. Of course, I had brought this torment on myself. I should have followed my father's maxim, "Pass things by," (in other words "Do not poke your nose into other people's business").

Boys assembled in the yard before proceeding to classes. Each class had a separate point in the schoolyard at which to queue before being led into class by its teacher.

Down to the left of my class photo were the toilets, an addendum to the East-West wing. These consisted of a smelly concrete channel, open to the weather, behind an outside front wall, into which the boys urinated, and which was sometimes disinfected with Jeyes Fluid. Behind this urinal-channel was a set of toilet chambers, usually in a disgusting condition.

So disgusting were the toilet bowls that I never actually used them in all my four years in the Boys' school, preferring to take my load home, which was only a few hundred yards from the school. On one occasion, when I was ill, I was allowed to use the Masters' toilet, which was indoors, sparklingly clean, and equipped with paper, but smelt of stale tobacco. There never was toilet paper in the boys' toilets, and we had a school-yard rhyme:

> "In this hall there is no paper,
> But, on the floor, you'll find a scraper.
> If the scraper can't be found,
> Just wipe your arse along the ground."

Of course, we did not use toilet paper at home either, except when we had visitors. Instead, yesterday's newspaper was cut into "squares," which were used for the purpose. If you wanted to use the school toilets, you should equip yourself first with newspaper cuttings.

We had a joke about a boy who was sent to buy toilet paper

when his family was about to have visitors. The shopkeeper, said, "You can have a pack of two rolls for five pence, or a pack of six rolls for a shilling." The boy was flummoxed: he asked, "Which is best?" And the shopkeeper said, "Well, on the whole it's all the same."

Most of our jokes were about Paddy the Irishman. He was marooned on a dessert island with Paddy the Englishman and Paddy the Scotchman. The only thing on the island was a dusty old lamp. Paddy the Irishman went to wipe the dust off the lamp, when a genie appeared, saying, "Paddy, you can have three wishes." Paddy the Irishman said, "I will let my two companions have a wish each, and then I will take the third wish." "That's OK with me, said the genie." So, Paddy the Scotchman said, "I miss the sound of the bagpipes; I wish I were back home in Lanarkshire." Then Paddy the Englishman said, "I miss the sound of the traffic; I wish I were back home in London," and Paddy the Irishman said, "I miss my two companions, Paddy the Scotchman and Paddy the Englishman; I wish they were back here with me."

Outside the toilet, there was a single brass tap protruding from the wall, over an outdoor sink, which provided water for the five hundred. You can guess that we did not wash hands very often after urinating.

This brass tap was to feature in one of my innovations in my last years in the school. One day, while the teacher was out of the room, my pal shot a paper pellet out of his "sling," (really a rubber-band catapult, hung between thumb and index-finger), which hit another student in the eye. The victim made a big whinge and teacher had him escorted to the Mater Hospital. It was found that no damage had been done, but the teachers decided to ban slings in the school, which were all the rage at the time.

Now, my problem was that I believed that my pals would obey the ban, but that the other side would not. I suspected that the other side would take advantage of our decommissioning to increase the level of their onslaught on us. So, I mulled over the possibility of a new scenario. I decided to introduce water-bombs to the school. These were unknown in Phibsborough, but my big brother, Roger, who had by now moved on to Secondary School, had been introduced to them in O'Connell's CBS.

If I were successful in my plan, I would completely change the schoolyard culture from slings to water-bombs.

Since I lacked courage myself, I decided to induce someone else to start using the water bombs. I called one of the other side, who had obvious leadership qualities, and said, "Hey; let me show you something."

I showed him how to fold a double copy-book-page to form a paper grenade, and how to fill the grenade from the tap. Then I lobbed the grenade at an innocent passer-by. Fortunately, my lob was accurate, and I gave the victim a good splash.

My apprentice bomb-maker was delighted. He launched into a water-bombing crusade, and soon water-bombs became the new rage in the schoolyard, and slings were forgotten. This was a very good outcome, but the teachers took a different view. They decided to ban water-bombs.

A Committee of two teachers was set up to go around all the classes, interrogating the whole school. They came into our class, swishing their bamboo canes, and demanded that the boy who had introduced water-bombs to the school stand up. I stayed mum, and the committee of teachers moved on to the next class.

At the next break, I approached the guy I had tutored and said, "I want to thank you for that."

He said, "For what?"

I said, "For not spilling the beans on how I brought in the water-bombs."

"You must be joking!" he said.

He had actually forgotten that I had shown him. Basking in the fame of being the innovator, he had come to believe that he himself had invented and introduced water-bombs.

I digress. Let me return to my first day in Big Boys' School.

There were two doors into the school buildings from the Boys' schoolyard: one at the top of a terrifying external iron stairs onto the main building; the second on ground level, leading to an internal stairwell in the secondary wing.

It was up the frightening iron stairs (originally intended as a fire-escape) that I and the other new Big Boys were shepherded. Once inside the door, we were directed down to the far end of the long corridor, into a very large room, which was soon pretty well filled by over a hundred boys.

Three tall teachers and one smaller, skinnier, man faced us in that room. The teachers were swishing bamboo canes to impress us with their authority.

The head teacher, Mr Lacy, soon quietened the crowd and explained to us, in no uncertain terms, that we would find Big School much different from the Junior School. There were no lady teachers in Senior School to mollycoddle us, nor was there to be any occasion for lounging or frolicking. There would be no marla (modelling-clay), no arts and crafts, no roly-poly, only hard work and lessons. And bamboo canes would be used to maintain order and to make sure lessons were learned.

Then Mr Lacy introduced the smaller man. This was Mr Lyons, the School Attendance Officer.

Mr Lyons said he would be visiting the school at regular intervals and inspecting the Roll Books. If he found that any students were mitching from school, he would have them arrested by the Gárdaí and brought to Artane Industrial School, where they would be kept under lock and key until they were fourteen years old, and where, not only would they have to do their lessons, but they would also have to do industrial work to pay for their upkeep.

Mr Lyons' talk was no idle threat. We were soon to learn from senior boys, in the school yard, of their former classmates who had been dragged away by the guards, roaring and screaming, and who could now, fully tamed, be seen playing in the Artane Boys Band on Sundays in Croke Park. We also heard that parents who were unable to control their children often "sent" them to Artane.

Nowadays, they think it horrible to make children do physical work. My father, however, reared on a small farm, believed in physical work as essential training for boys. So, in addition to our household chores at home, my brothers and I were brought to Glasnevin regularly to help on his vegetable plot, (one of Dublin Corporation Allotments situated in the area where the Claremont and Clareville housing estates are now). Dad took two of us on his bicycle to the plot, one on the crossbar and the other on the carrier behind the saddle, until we were old enough to cycle ourselves, which was very soon after each started Big Boys' School. (Of course, all this work was good fun, and he also took us to the park to play football and teach us hurling. Plots on Saturdays, park on Sundays!)

As regards Corporal Punishment, my father thought this was a necessary tool of child-rearing. He believed the motto of his age, "Spare the rod and spoil the child," and used a leather strap to keep discipline at home.

Mr Lyons took his leave, and Mr O'Connor was given the floor.

It was explained to us that Mr O'Connor was going to call out names of about half the boys in the room. Those whose names were called were, then, to follow Mr O'Connor to another room, while the rest were to remain in this room (with Mr Piggott). Somebody whispered that Piggy would be best, because O'Connor was a demon with the cane. I was surprised that any one of us would have such knowledge, and it was a kind of little epiphany for me to realise that there are others, in any environment, who will be more informed than me as to what is happening.

Over 50 names were called out, including mine. We fifty-or-so then followed Mr O'Connor to his class-room, which was on the short corridor, after the principal's telephone-box-sized office, and obliquely overlooked Dalymount Park.

Classmates recall Mr O'Connor allowing us to watch, from the class-room windows, an international soccer match, with a Communist country, that had been banned by Archbishop John Charles McQuaid. I remember occasionally having opportunity of viewing a match from the windows, but never found them interesting from that distance or oblique angle, or at all, and I never struggled for a position at a window.

Dalymount Park was usually made available to the school for its annual sports day. When not available, we used Birmingham's Farm, off Connaught Street, which has since become Mount Bernard Park.

At the sports, I once almost won the sack race, but fell just a yard short of the finish. Another year I did win the three-legged race with my companion Rooney Galvin. We each got a jar of brylcreem for our prize.

When we entered Mr O'Connor's class-room that first day, Mossy, (as we soon dared call Mr O'Connor, but not to his face), ordered us to stand around the walls of the room, behind the rows of desks.

Mr O'Connor then called out names again, one by one, placing us in our assigned desks, each desk being a two-seater. When we were all seated, he explained that we were arranged in streams, the boys who had been rated brightest to our left, the ones who would have to work hardest to the right, and the in-betweeners in between.

Next task was to give us all our new names, for we were entered in the Roll Book under the Irish form of our name.

I became Proinnsias Ó Cillín (instead of Francis Killeen). Much later in life, children playing in the street were to miss-pronounce "Proinnsias" as "Krunchie," which I have adopted as a pen-name.

Mossy O'Connor had placed me at the bottom end of the first rank, beside the person I sat beside in Junior School, i.e., Paddy Monahan. Paddy was a jolly fellow, but not an ideal desk companion, for he was full of fun, and sometimes made it difficult to pay attention to teacher.

In the previous year he had made up a war game, where two persons marked out the movement of their armies on paper. It might have worked as a computer game, if there were such a thing as a computer, but it was not satisfactory as a paper game. When you played that game with Paddy, it was so contrived that Paddy had to win. So I wrote a little poem about it, (my first ever poem), that Paddy did not like at all. The poem goes:

> I'll tell you a story
> About Paddy Baloney
> Who sits beside me in school.
>
> He's very barmy;
> He's got an army
> Drawn on paper with pencil and rule.

If you sit down beside him,
You'll have to fight him,
With you own pencilled army, of course.

The game is a fiddle;
You must march down the middle,
So Paddy can outflank your force.

If you protest,
I do not jest,
Paddy will insist it's the rule.

Whatever the weather,
Paddy's the winner.
And his foe is always the fool.

I can tell you that the poem took a big effort (and a heightened mental state), and that I spent an entire weekend writing it out. I brought my creation into school on Monday morning and attempted to read it out to Paddy. I thought he would be amused, but he said, "That's rubbish." Disappointed, I threw the poem into the waste paper basket.

It is not very remarkable that I should attempt to compose a poem at seven-and-a-half, for, as I have found through parenting, children of that age, or even a bit younger, often burst into a poetry-writing phase. What is remarkable is that I had so competently mastered the physical skill of writing. This was under the tutelage of my teacher in Junior School, Mrs Finucane, Marian Finucane's mother, who walked around the class supervising our writing and tapping, with her ruler, the knuckles of any child who was holding the pencil incorrectly.

One of the surprises for me that first day in Big Boys' School was that my next door neighbour, Dessie Breen, was also in my class. Dessie was almost a year older than me and had started Big Boys School the previous year. His parents held him back, because they thought he was too young for his previous class.

The three bigger Breen boys and the three Killeen boys, with a few others, used to gather in a make-shift den at the bottom of Breen's garden. There we would play cards, conkers, jack-stones and marbles, sing songs, and discuss politics and life. All our songs were borrowed, so some-one suggested we should make up our own. Dessie composed a song and presented it at one of our gatherings. We were not too impressed, and the song was not adopted. (I said it sounded makey-up). It is actually very hard to compose an anthem that does not sound corny, and most Eurovision entries and many pop-songs also sound makey-up.

A general election took place in England at this time, and Winston Churchill came back as Prime Minister (October 1951). My father used to read the paper out loud at meal-times, and now quoted speculation that Churchill might try to "take back the ports." If so, the Norfolk Boys (with exaggerated idea of our own military ability) were willing to play our part in national resistance. One day we resolved, (for fun and games rather than with serious military intent), to change the name of our little society from "Norfolk Boys Association," to "Norfolk Boys Army." Roger Killeen was appointed Commander-in-chief (subject to the Council of

War consisting of the entire membership) and we waged a successful war against the boys of the Tramway Cottages.

One of our songs was *Kevin Barry*:

> "... British soldiers tortured Barry,
> Just because he would not tell
> The names of his companions
> And other things they wished to know ..."

I raised the question in the den as to what we would do if, in the event of a national resistance, we were captured and questioned. Dessie said he would tell lies to the interrogators. I disagreed, as, in my view, the only effective strategy would be to say nothing at all.

Churchill's threat passed, and, in the heel of the hunt, despite our boyhood enthusiasm for national defence, only one of the Keyhole boys, Paddy Breen, when old enough, was ever to join the volunteer defence force, the FCA (Fórsa Cosanta Áitiúil).

Several of us were, however, already in the Order of Malta, a voluntary first-aid organisation, usually referred to as the "Knights of Malta." We attended classes where we learned first-aid, and went from house to house collecting weekly subscriptions to fund our uniforms. When we got our uniforms, we took part in parades all over Dublin.

I did very well at pretend first-aid sessions, but not so well in the real world. I disliked being on hazard for sickness and injury, and I disliked being in uniform, with everybody gawking at me. Attending men's football matches in uniform, I felt bullied by the injured men, who refused to lie down for treatment, but grabbed my water-bottle or dettol for self-medication, and jumped back into the field of fray without waiting for wound-cleaning and banding. One evening I partnered an adult member of the Knights in the New Electric Cinema, on Talbot Street, where there often was a fracas, sometimes with knives (but nothing happened on my night). My father refused to let me volunteer for that duty again. (He only let me go on my first stint because I had already given my word).

We remained in the Knights of Malta for several years. One of the rewards of exemplary service was selection to assist in a pilgrimage to Lourdes. In 1954, my brother Jerry was selected, and I was chosen to go in 1955. I didn't like the idea of parading around in uniform in torch-lit processions, or of dipping in ice-cold water, or wheeling sick people around, or all the medals and holy pictures, or funny French food; so I made my excuses and stayed at home.

Let's get back to Mossy O'Connor's classroom, on my first day in Big Boys' School. Dessie Breen started this new school year at the top place in the class-room. During the next few years, as Mossy applied his own assessment to the streaming, I was gradually to move up from the bottom to the top of the first rank, and soon enough would be sitting beside Dessie. Then Dessie was to drop back a desk or two.

Paddy Spain was one of the boys in the seat in front of me on day one. I remember this, because of a remark he made that his father decried Compulsory Irish. In response, I retorted, "What about compulsory English, Compulsory Maths, Compulsory Religious Doctrine, and so on?" for, as far as we kids were concerned, all subjects were compulsory.

This exchange underlines a difference in attitude (reflecting parental views) over one of the emerging contentious issues of the day: how the national desire to enhance our cultural, as well as economic, independence from England, by promoting the Irish Language, placed an onerous educational burden on individuals and, perhaps, used resources that could be put to more practical objectives.

Earlier that year, there had been a General Election in Ireland. After Mass, one Sunday, a political rally was held outside St. Peter's Church.

I remember an intense, young candidate, Declan Costello of Fine Gael, standing on the platform and declaring, "'Bread and Butter' is all that Matters." (Actually what he said was "'Bread and Butter' is what matters," but I prefer to remember the first version). It is peculiar that this sticks in my memory. I joined a bunch of kids marching up Saint Peter's Road singing,

> "Starvation once again;
> Starvation once again;
> No bread, no butter,
> No tea, no sugar;
> Starvation once again."

I suppose "'Bread and Butter' is what matters" is a paraphrase for "It's the economy, stupid." Despite this being the issue of the day, the economy continued in decline, with massive emigration.

For me, and for children of teachers, civil servants and bank officials, the prospects of employment in Ireland were reasonably good, for our home environment ensured we could aspire for similar positions ourselves. Some other classmates had reasonable prospects: Dessie Breen's dad was a member of a printer's union, which preserved jobs for family members; Paddy Spain's dad could bring him into the family business (furniture-making and upholstery); Paddy Reilly had reasonable expectations of following his dad into Guinness', and there were, no doubt, other examples of this kind.

For many of the boys in the class, however, the prospect of employment in Ireland was grim, and they knew it. The country was in depression and decline. Their fathers were unemployed or worked in "dead-end" or casual jobs. Industrial wages, which were already low after "the economic war" of the 1930s, had actually fallen during the recent World War. It is not surprising that there was a general atmosphere of disaffection and cynicism.

When Dublin Corporation made vegetable plots available, during the war years, in Glasnevin, they were not taken up by the unemployed, but rather by Civil Servants, Guards and Teachers, using their spare time. The unemployed and insecure workers regarded voluntary effort as denying work to the unemployed, as well as putting their dole, and associated benefits, at risk, (as the turf delivery men were to find out).

One day, Mossy asked "all those whose father is out of work" to stand up. On that day, my father happened to be in hospital to have varicose veins removed, so I stood up, along with, I suppose, about a third of the class. Mossy looked at me and said, "Sit down, Killeen."

Those who stood up were to get a small bottle of milk (1/3 of a pint) and a sandwich every day. This scheme varied from year to year. Mostly, it was open to all the students, but, at other times, cutbacks limited it to children of the unemployed. On Mondays and Wednesdays we had cheese sambos, Tuesdays and Thursdays brawn, and Fridays a currant bun.

An attitudinal study of my classmates would find that the majority were generous, cooperative, fair-minded and sharing, but that there was a substantial minority who were mean, clique-ish and acquisitive. While the first group was reared to ask "what can I do," the second was focused on: "what can I get?"

"Finders Keepers, Losers Seekers," was a motto applied as well as enunciated. Many classmates considered it legitimate to keep items found. Nor had an item to be irretrievably lost – it only needed to be left lying around without supervision. So, if you wanted to keep your possessions, you had to mind them.

Some of the boys boasted of using the "Free Counter," meaning lifting things from shops like Woolworth's, without paying. Surplus goods thus acquired were often swapped and bartered in class and in the schoolyard.

Many of the kids had money to buy chips. When I asked at home to have real (chip-shop) chips for dinner, my father asked: "How much does a single of chips cost?" I replied what the price was, and he said, "You could get a stone of potatoes in Neville's shop for that. Chips are clearly a waste of money. You can have fried potatoes instead, which are just as good." Fried potatoes were a re-hash of boiled potatoes, sliced and then fried on the pan. Tasty as they were, they were not chips!

Given the cultural differences in my class-room, it is not surprising that my best friend was to be a boy from a similar background to my own – Rooney Galvin, one of four brothers, whose parents were from the country and whose father, a teacher, had fought in the War of Independence and, like my father, had taken on a vegetable plot in Glasnevin. The Galvin brothers were friends with the Killeen brothers, and often visited each other's houses.

Mossy O'Connor, the teacher, from rural Ireland himself (County Kerry), shared an outlook like my parents. He gave up his spare time to organise the school's football and hurling teams, as well as serving voluntarily on the committee of the *Primary Schools League*. Besides being a strong supporter of Gaelic games and the Irish Language and culture, I remember him as favouring *Clann na Poblachtda* economic policies, such as *Afforestation* and *Import Substitution*. (My father, however, was cynical about protectionism, which he thought was unconscionably exploited by businessmen who charged excessive prices for poor-quality goods). By the time I left Primary School, I had come to believe that it would be wiser for the government to develop Ireland as a hub of trade; I was before my time. Mossy's enthusiasm and even his constant use of the bamboo cane were to fail to evoke positive nationalism in his pupils, in the cynical climate of the fifties. He did, however, evoke enthusiasm for football and hurling.

The first day that Mossy took the class to the Phoenix Park to play football, he hired a coach. This was so that we would know in future where to go, in the park. On all subsequent occasions, we had to make our own way. The playing fields in the Phoenix Park are about three miles from the school. There was no public "active open space," in which to play football, in Phibsborough or Cabra. Of course, we played football, hurling, cricket, and, occasionally, rounders, on the road, all to street rules.

In the schoolyard one day, my brother Roger, three years older than me, introduced me to the school's champion footballer. We were due to play in the semi-final against Ringsend, a team with a very tough reputation. I asked the champion if we stood a chance. He said, "We'll bit the shit out of them."

I thought Mossy's use of the cane was fair and reasonable. One particular boy got caned every day, but this was because he was incorrigible in disobeying a simple instruction. He always drew the margin on his copy book freehand, instead of using a Ruler, as instructed. He could have avoided the caning simply by using some straight object to draw his margin.

The lash of a cane gave a sharp pain, but this was external and short-lasting, not like a migraine or a toothache, and hurt a lot less than a disparaging remark.

Mossy had a number of techniques for waking up a somnolent class. One was to open the windows wide and let a great blast of cold air into the room. Another was to march the entire class down the stairs into the yard to do physical exercises. A third was to order us out of our desks, to stand around the walls of the room, whereupon he would throw a question at each one in turn, with cane in hand to strike the hand of anyone who gave a wrong answer.

I, of course, never really deserved a caning myself, unlike my classmates, but was pleased to receive the occasional lash of the cane, so as not to be differentiated from the others.

How should you respond to a caning? I shared the view of my classmates that a worthy boy would not flinch or whinge when caned. He would stand erect and show no pain or emotion. Teachers, however, wanted the punished child to show some form of remorse. So, on one occasion when I showed indifference to a light punishment, Mossy responded by giving me six of the best on each hand. I can understand the teacher's attitude. While we thought that a show of indifference was an act of courage, teachers saw it as impudence.

I do not recall Mossy ever punishing anybody for playing foreign games (as happened in Christian Brothers' schools). However, I have met an ex-pupil, of a later class, who says he and a pal were punished by Mossy for taking part in the Cabra Soccer Streets' League (but, technically, for using the school name without authority). By this man's account, Mossy referred the two soccer-players to Mr Nevin for a severe caning. Mr Nevin, known as "Killer," was able to apply the cane more forcefully than anyone else.

Soccer was more suitable than Gaelic football for street play (since the ball could be kept low), so, outside of school, it was more popular. This was the choice of the choirboys and the Knights of Malta (whose membership overlapped), on their outings.

While the Breens, next door, were in the Scouts, the Killeens were choir boys. (I wanted to join the scouts, but was not allowed. I gather that my father, who trusted priests and teachers, was not so sure of scout masters). We usually had choir practice on Tuesdays and Thursdays at 7.30 pm. Paddy Somerville, Jerry's school-teacher, the choir-master, had the key of the boys' stairs, so we entered by the Infants' or Girls' door, and proceeded up the internal stone stairs to Paddy Somerville's class-room. Father Vincent Allen was chaplain of the choir, as well as being manager of the school, and he had control of the key.

Mass in those days was in Latin, and I had the pleasure of taking part in choir performances of some very beautiful songs: motets by Palestrina and Mozart, as well as Benedictine Plain Chant. My favourite motet was *Regina Coeli,* by Antonio Lotti, sung on Easter Sunday at 12 mid-day to a packed church. All during lent, the great organ had been silent. On Easter Sunday, as the congregation entered the church, the choir assembled silently in the gallery, about 12 men and 50 boys. No whispering, but treading softly, softly, as we took up our positions. The opening note was generated quietly by tuning fork and passed around. The conductor raised his two hands, holding the attention of all, and then suddenly the silence was broken by the explosive sound of the choir at full voice, supported by the organ at full volume; and the words, "Regina Coeli, Laetare Allelulia" ("Queen of Heaven, Rejoice, Alleluia") burst out thunderously. Nobody has ever equalled our version. The song can be heard on YouTube by searching "Antonio Lotti Regina Coeli;" however, never as strong and surprising as ours!

St Peter's Church Choir was probably the second best church choir in Dublin. The *Palestrina Choir*, attached to the Pro-Cathedral, was reckoned to be the best. They poached members from the other choirs around the city. My brother, Roger, was a beautiful soprano, as was his mate Robert Higgs, and both of these were recruited into the *Palestrina Choir*, to the detriment of St Peter's. Bobby had leukaemia, and was to die in his teens.

As well as singing at Christmas and Easter, and some other Feast Days, we sang at Benediction after 12 o'clock Mass every Sunday (except during the school's Summer holidays). After lunch we would meet the choir-boys again in the Phoenix Park for a game of football. The game was Soccer, except that a team was not limited to eleven players, but consisted of as many as turned up divided into two teams.

One day in the Phoenix Park, I was shot.

Some boys from Cabra West were having fun throwing their weight around. One of them had an air-gun, and it was with this that I was shot. Fortunately, he was some distance away; and the pellet, which hit me in the fleshy base of the thumb, while it gave me a sharp pain, did not have enough force to do much damage. Did we stand up to the Cabra Kids and fight back? No, we fled the scene; there were only a handful of us there that day.

The full list of teachers in the Big Boys' School, to the best of my memory, at the time, was: Mr Piggott, Mr Sullivan, Mr Somerville, (my brother, Jerry's, teacher), Mr Nevin and Mr Lacy, in the long corridor; and Mr O'Shea, Mr O'Brien, (my brother, Roger's, teacher), Mr Woods and Mr O'Connor, in the short corridor, nine teachers in all. There must have been two classes at each standard, making eight classes, and, in addition, Mr Woods took the pupils who stayed on after sixth standard to wait for their 14th birthday, when they would no longer be obliged by law to go to school.

Not all teachers were zealots like Mossy O'Connor. He alone looked after all the hurling and football, giving up his free time. This meant he did not have time for lucrative side-lines that other teachers took up. He remained single, so had more free time for ball games than the married teachers. Other teachers were often less energetic in the class-room, bringing less passion into the work, some never even using the cane at all. The end result was that all of Mossy's boys passed the Primary Examination, while there were multiple failures in some other classes. I would rather have the disciplinarian and succeed than the soft teacher and fail.

Many of the songs I play and sing to this day (for example, in Clareville Centre at lunch-hour on Thursdays), are songs I learned in Mossy O'Connor's class.

If each of nine teachers had a class of 50 boys, there must have been about 450 boys in the school. How did we all fit in the little school yard? We were let out to the toilets one class at a time, to prevent a rush on the facilities. In general, assembling for school, we milled around the school yard until the bell rang, and did not consider it cramped or small at the time.

At the end of our first day in Big School, we were severely warned against running on the corridor or tussling on the stairs. When the school-bell rang, one class would be released at a time, to avoid accidents on the stairs.

The classes on the long corridor were obliged to use the terrifying iron stairs, but, fortunately, our class, being on the short corridor, was to use the internal, stone stairs.

On the stairs, I got the fright of my life. Andrew Eager (not his real name), a sturdy boy, much heavier than me, began to push me around and impose himself on me. I had read enough comics to know that if you submitted to a bully, your life would be hell, and it would be very hard to get out of it. I drew the awful conclusion that I had to take decisive action here and now to stop this potential bullying at the very beginning.

From my experience of nose-bleeds, I believed that the nose is a vulnerable part. As Andy pushed and poked me, I focused on his nose, and when he pulled back a little bit from me, giving me room, I swung my right fist with every ounce of strength I could muster. I landed a whopper right smack on the side of his nose, which instantly spouted blood.

As Andy stumbled back in shock and surprise, I calmly stepped down the stairs, out into the schoolyard, across the yard to the gate, up the lane and home.

I guess now the reason Andy had a go at me was that he

was extremely stressed after the first day's treatment in senior school, and chose me as a random vulnerable target on which to release his pent-up anger.

When I arrived home, my mother cried: "O Francie, you have been fighting! Look at the state of you."

I said: "You should see the state of the other fellow!"

You can rest assured that Andrew Eager never troubled me again.

Killeen, Krunchie

One Tea Bag

One tea bag can furnish
Many cups of tea.
That they waste so many
Is a cause of concern to me.

Too often I see them
Throw the bag away,
After it has furnished
A single cup of tay.

Please take the tea bag out
After a count of two;
And hang it up to dry
Like civil servants do.

Hang it up and use it
At the next tea break:
And see how many cups
One tea bag can make.

Don't leave the tea bag in
Till the tea is thick as tar.
Dip it in and take it out
For a better cup by far.

Then you can enjoy that bag,
Again and again.

Green Label, I have found,
Can make up to ten.

And, when the flavour's all used up,
Still don't let it go.
Assign it to the compost heap
To help your garden grow.

Lyons, Maura

One Boy and his Dog

"Honestly, dad, just have a look at him: he is a fine cut of a dog – and has lovely brown eyes and a shiny brown coat."

"Is that so?" Johnny said, his mouth turned down, his nerves at breaking point; "Will you for God's sake wake up, you bloody Idiot."

"But, dad," Thomas said: "Just keep him for a few days: he will not need much. We can put up a bed in the porch for him," (which is near the back door in the council house).

Johnny ran his hands through his thinning brown hair. He wondered how he was going to feed his eight children with more than a boiled egg and mashed potatoes, which was all he could afford on his small pension.

How he wished his wife Rosie, their mother, was still here to look after them; and he had to keep going even though many a day he just wanted to get drunk and run away.

When Rosie died in childbirth, his world had collapsed.

"OK, I am fed-up arguing with you. Where is this fine cut of a dog you have fallen in love with?"

Thomas grinned, his red hair shining and his blue eyes full of mischief. He knew how to get around dad: all you had to do was keep the story going and squeeze a few tears out of the eye.

After all, he could hardly have left the dog all alone in the mountains – where he and another boy had found him. They had words and the deal had been done. The boy wanted the jar of blackberries and Thomas wanted the dog.

Thomas opened the front door, and Johnny followed, thinking it would cost a fortune to feed the dog he had agreed to look after, which now followed them into the kitchen.

"All we have to do, dad, is put an ad in the paper," thinking there was sure to be a good reward.

Thomas loved all animals and always would.

He decided to call the dog "Shep."

Johnny read the paper.

"Lord," he thought. "It's all bad news these days."

He turned his paper to the last page, and there this ad was.

"Well," Johnny said, coming in with the newspaper under his arm, "You got your way, Thomas, now it's my turn. I want you all to do what I tell you. Maura, you can sit at the parlour window. Cathleen, you can also join Maura at the window. As soon as you see a fancy car pulling up, give me the billy-o, so that I can put on my new waistcoat and have a drop of the auld stuff ready to greet our visitor."

"He's here, he's here," said Maura to Cathleen, as the fancy car pulled up outside the window.

Michael sat at the kitchen window. Sean stood up against

the wall. Noel sat at the table eating bread and jam.

Michael said, "This is my dad."

Thomas stood by the open window. Johnny said, "Come In, come in," as the stranger knocked on the door.

"Sure it's great to see you," said Johnny, as the visitor walked in the door.

"You are a good man, anyone can see that," as Johnny and the stranger walked into the kitchen, "We have all looked after him and will miss him, especially the children."

"You have my thanks; my dog has been missing for a week. I'm glad to see he is looking well, and the kids love him obviously; so I have decided you can keep him; he has been eating me out of house and home."

He opened the window and jumped out.

Sean and Noel followed. The rest of them did nothing.

"Well, that's that," Johnny said, as he opened the front door gulping the rest of the whiskey (he drank the stranger's glass as well).

The dog was the last to jump out of the window. There was no longer the boy and his dog,

Lyons, Maura

It's Not All About Money

Maura tidied the shelves, her blue eyes sweeping about the charity shop she volunteered to help in two afternoons a week. There was little left to do and less left to sell.

It was Christmas Eve, and after a hectic past few weeks in the shop, with its cheery Christmas Tree in a corner, and garlands of holly and ivy decorating the walls and hung from the ceiling, she was wondering if the snowflakes that fell from early morning that Friday would last over the Christmas.

Suddenly the front door flew open with a clang, bringing with it a gust of cold air that wrapped itself around her legs.

A man in his late twenties stood facing her, his curly red hair covered in snow flakes and his face flushed red with the cold. He had parked a white van with the name of a local builder outside the shop, which stood on a corner of the small seaside town.

"Sorry Lady!" the man said, his eyes darting from the empty shelves to the almost empty shop window, "I hope I didn't frighten you; but I'm in such a mess, I've been all over the town looking for presents for my three kids, but it looks like I have left everything too late."

The man's voice broke and he burst into tears, asking Maura what was he going to tell the misses who would surely kill him.

Maura looked up at the clock on the shop wall. It was almost 2.30.

Nancy, the shop manageress, had gone to do the banking and would be back by 3.00. The plan was to meet up with the other two volunteers, Rose and Alice, for a Christmas drink in the nearby public house. Called the Queen Bess, the Tudor Era styled pub was packed with mums and dads all laden down with parcels and presents of all shapes and sizes. Her mind raced watching the young man pacing the floor.

Maura made a decision. After all it was Christmas.

Surely, she told herself, when those soldiers who were based at the nearby Army Barracks, located a few miles away from the popular seaside town, had loaded all those lovely Christmas toys into the huge lorry that had arrived at the shop, too late to be priced up in time for the Christmas rush, had in mind, she believed, somebody just like her upset customer.

"No time for whinging," Maura told the man.

Taking his arm she directed him to the stairs leading down to the storerooms at the bottom of the shop.

On reaching the basement level, the man let out a gasp of surprise and wonderment.

"It's like Aladdin's Cave down here," he said.

His face lit up and, with like an astonished laugh, looked at the many bikes and doll's prams and other children's toys that lay scattered about. They were all un-priced and in no kind of order.

The man had two girls aged 8 and 5 and a boy of 2. His problem was solved.

The Policeman who had kept his eye on things going on in the charity shop, was delighted, as usual, to help get the toys, a dolls pram a train set, a shop that was turned into either a hairdresser's or a beauty salon or a sweet shop at the touch of a button, and several bags of sweets, and also many colouring books and a huge football, into the very grateful man's van.

The man paid Maura all the money he had left after his visit to a pub and a quick bet at the bookies; it totalled £15, all in coins.

Maura handed the cash to Nancy on her Return to the shop, just as the white van disappeared out of sight amid a blur of snowflakes.

On hearing the full story, with a smile on her face Nancy assured Maura that Christmas or Charity was not all about money and never would be.

Myers, Patricia

A Touch of Magic

This is a work of fiction. Any resemblance to actual persons, living or dead, is entirely coincidental.

"Timmy; it's seven thirty, time to get up for school."

June Smyth sighed; she looked at her three year old daughter, smiling up at her.

"OK, Amanda, I'll get your breakfast. Timmy, come on; you don't want to be late."

"I'm coming; stop yelling!"

"I am not yelling; here's your breakfast."

"Don't want any."

"Please, Timmy, you must eat something."

"Are you deaf? I don't want any!"

"Don't you talk to me like that, I am your mum."

"Oh shut up!"

With that he stormed out of the house

Later, while Amanda was playing, June sat down at the table. Tears running down her face, she thought to herself, "What am I going to do?"

"Hello, June!"

It's Lisa. The door was open.

Seeing her friend in such a state shocked her. She rushed to June, putting her arms around her, saying, "June, what's wrong? Has something happened?"

"Oh, Lisa!. It's Timmy. He's changed so much; I don't know what to do any more. June, his Dad left almost a year ago, and in all that time, has he said anything about that? No! And I can see the anger in him; sometimes, when he looks at me, I can see the hate he has for me in his eyes. He blames me."

"Why would he blame you?"

"I don't know; this morning he would not eat; told me to shut up, and slammed out."

"June, have you given any thought to getting counselling for Timmy?"

"I've thought about it, but I don't know if he'd go."

"For God's sake, June, he's only eleven years old; he'll have to do as you say. You think he has changed so much, its frightening."

"Oh, there's the phone! Hello!"

"Mrs Smyth, this is Tom Madison, I'm Timmy's head teacher."

"Oh, has something happened to Timmy?"

"No he's fine, but I would like to talk to you. Can you come and see me, please?"

"Yes, I'll come now; I should be there in thirty minutes."

"Fine; I'll see you then."

"Lisa, that was the principal of Tim's school. He wants to see me; can you watch Amanda for me?"

"Of course; you go ahead."

Arriving at the school, she took a deep breath and went to the principal's office. Feeling apprehensive, she knocked on the door.

"Come in!"

"Hello! I'm June Smyth, Timmy's mum, what's wrong? Has he been hurt?"

"No; nothing like that. I'm afraid I had to send Timmy to detention."

"Why; what has he done?"

"Mrs Smyth, we have had a lot of complaints about him, both from his teachers and some parents."

"Complaints?"

"Timmy has been giving a lot of abuse to his teachers, and he's also started to bully some of his school friends. As a matter of fact, he spends a lot of his time alone now. I'm afraid the other boys won't have anything to do with him."

Sitting with her head down, not knowing where to look or what to do, she said:

"Mr Madison, I don't know what to say."

"Mrs Smyth, has anything happened at home? You see, I've noticed a big change in Tim over the last seven or eight months."

Shaking with shock she told him:

"Tim's father left us about a year ago without a word. I don't know why he left; I came back from shopping, and he was just gone."

"I hear what you are saying, Mrs Smyth. It's what you are not saying that troubles me."

"Please, Mr Madison, let's leave it. I promise I'll talk to Timmy tonight."

"Very well; we'll leave it at that. Take care of yourself."

"Goodbye, Mr Madison; thank you."

Back at home, June told Lisa what had happened.

"You're going to have to talk to him; this has gone on long enough."

"I will do it tonight after Amanda has gone to bed."

"I have to go now June. If you need me, just ring."

Later that evening, when Amanda had gone to bed, she

called Timmy.

"What do you want? I'm going to bed."

"Timmy, get down here now, I want to talk to you."

Coming down from his room, he threw himself into the chair.

"Well, I'm here. What do you want?"

"What has happened to you, Tim? You used to be a happy little boy, always up to mischief, always laughing. Please talk to me. Mr Madison sent for me today. He said you were abusive to the teachers, and bullying some of the students."

"I did not bully anyone. I hit one or two; they asked for it."

"Oh god, Tim, what am I going to do with you?"

"Maybe you would like to drive me out like you did dad."

"What? I did not drive your father out. He left us of his own free will."

"No! You're lying; he would not leave us. Damn you. I hate you. I hate you!"

Running to his room, he fell on his bed and cried.

Downstairs June sat in shock.

"Dear god, what am I going to do?"

It was a while later she realised her phone was ringing.

"Hello!"

"Hello, June, it's Lisa. Are you alright?"

"No, I'm not."

"I guess it did not go well with Tim."

"You guess right, and now I'm going to have to get a job of some kind, the bills are getting too hard to cope with."

"How are you going to work?"

"Well, Tim is in school and I could try and get Amanda into Pre School. If I could get something between nine thirty and one thirty, at least it would help with the bills."

"June, listen. I have a friend who runs a crèche. She was telling me the other day that she might be looking for someone; so leave it with me and I'll give her a ring tomorrow."

"Thank you, Lisa; I don't know what I would do without you."

"That's what friends are for. By the way, have you heard from David since he left?"

"Not one word; nothing."

"We will talk tomorrow. I have to go now; try and get some rest; good night!"

When Lisa was gone, she went upstairs to check on the children. Amanda was sleeping peacefully, like a little angel.

Closing the door softly, she went into Timmy's room. He was asleep. His face was streaked from his tears, his fists clenched tightly.

Kneeling down at his bed she prayed for help.

Next morning it was the same, Tim fighting her every step of the way.

"Timmy, come on: time for school."

Putting Amanda into her buggy, they left the house. Dragging his feet, he walked behind her. Looking around, he noticed his one time friend, Billy, passing by in his father's car.

I wonder where my daddy is; why did he leave us?

Looking at his mum: she drove him away, I hate her!

All these thoughts were going around and around in his head as he walked along.

When they reached the gates of the school, June bent down to kiss her son but he pushed her away, turning to his little sister he put his arms around her,

"See you later, sis." Then he went in the gates.

Watching all this was Mr Madison. He felt pity for Tim and his mum. He watched her walk away, her face drawn with sadness and worry, and wondered how he could help.

Later that day, he saw a chance to speak to Timmy.

"How are you, Tim?"

"I'm ok sir!"

"Tim, I'm sorry I had to send for your mum, but, as principal, I had no choice."

"Yes sir!"

"Tim, you seem very unhappy. Is there anything I can do to help?"

"I don't want any help, and I don't care that you told my mum; everything sucks anyway."

"Look, Tim, I'm a very good listener. If you want to talk ..."

"Talk about what?"

"Whatever is troubling you!"

"There is nothing wrong. School is over. I don't have to talk to you anymore."

As he watched the lad walk away, Mr Madison wished he could help, but knew in his heart he could not push Tim.

Walking through the park, Tim sat down on a bench, not in any hurry to go home. He felt something at his feet. Looking down, he saw there was a dog sitting there looking at him.

"What do you want, dog?"

The dog was wagging his tail. He seemed to want to play.

"Go away, you stupid dog," Tim shouted.

Getting up from the bench, Tim started for home. As he walked along, he heard something behind him. Stopping, he turned; and there was the dog,

"I told you to go away."

He started to throw stones at him shouting, "I told you to go away," and then the dog was gone.

When Tim arrived home, he was surprised to see the dog at the front door. Before he could say anything, his mum opened the door.

"Tim, what has kept you? I was worried."

"Nothing! I came home through the park."

"You know I don't like you doing that; there's so many bad people in the world."

"Yes, and you are one of them."

Shaking her head, she asked him, where the dog came from.

"Don't know, he was in the park and then he was here."

"Well, we had better give him something to eat and drink, he must belong to someone."

"I told you I don't know. He has no collar, and I don't want him in here."

"Very well, Tim. I'll feed him outside."

"Mum, phone, mum, phone!"

"I'm coming, Amanda. Hello."

"June, Lisa here! You start that job on Monday."

"Oh Lisa, that's great, thank you so much."

"Not a bother, I'll call over later if that's all right."

"Please do; I'll be glad to see you. Until later then! Goodbye. Tim, have you done your homework?"

"No; not doing it."

"Please. Tim. Not tonight! I can't have another night of arguments."

"You won't. I'm going to bed."

Sighing, she picked up Amanda:

"Time for your bath, young lady!"

Later, when the children were asleep, Lisa arrived.

"Hi, Lisa! I'm glad to see you, and thanks for helping me get that job."

"No problem; that's what friends are for. By the way, where did the dog come from?"

"I don't know, he followed Tim home; but Tim doesn't want him."

"Well, whether he wants him or not, the dog just went up

to his room."

"You know, Lisa, I'm too tired to care."

"Is Tim causing trouble again?"

"Indeed! He's so angry. I'm sorry, Lisa. Forgive my manners, would you like a glass of wine?"

"I thought you would never ask. June, why don't you tell him about his dad?"

"Tell him what, Lisa? That his dad is an alcoholic; that he hurt me? What good would that do? He adores his dad."

"For God's sake, June! It might teach him that not everything is black and white in this world. There are a lot of grey areas."

"You're probable right, but I'll have to wait until the time is right."

"Don't wait too long. After all, it's been nearly a year. It's not fair on Tim or you."

After Lisa left, June went up to bed herself. She thought over what Lisa had said.

"Dear God, help me do the right thing?"

She thought about the way Tim was a year ago; happy; always laughing; never a bad word from his mouth. Where had it all gone wrong? Tossing and turning, she finally fell into a troubled sleep.

Next morning, she awoke to Amanda laughing.

Going to her daughter's room, she found it empty. Running down the stairs, she was surprised to find Amanda playing with the dog.

Tim, hearing the noise, came down too. Seeing the dog, he said, "What's he doing here?"

"He got in when Lisa called around."

Tim looked but said nothing.

That weekend went quietly.

Monday arrived, and the same problems with it.

"Tim, please lift Amanda up to the table. I can't be late today."

"You're in a hurry; can't wait to get rid of me? Is that it?"

"Tim, look! I start work this morning. I need to get you to school. Amanda will be in the same créche where I'll be working."

"Why are you going to work?"

"Because we need the money now! Hurry up; and give the dog food and water."

"Where is the pooch? I can't see him. I guess he got tired of this house, just like dad."

"Tim, please! Not today!"

Getting to the school, Tim was surprised to see the dog already there.

"Where did you get to this morning? Not that I care!"

Woof, Woof.

"The same to you, pooch."

Timmy, looking around, saw Mr Madison.

"Hurry now, or you'll be late for class."

Tim sighed and said, "Yes sir."

Tom Madison bent down to rub the dog.

"Well dog, you seem to have taken a shine to Timmy. He needs a friend; so hang in there. What is it about you? I seem to know you! I must be losing it! I'm sitting here talking to a dog. Well, I'd better go now, before my students think I've taken the day off."

Laughing to himself, he went into the school.

"Hello; I'm June Smyth. My friend Lisa told me to come today."

"Welcome! I'm Nora Bell, and this must be Amanda. Come; I'll show you the room Amanda will be in, and then I'll tell you your duties. The children Amanda's age are in this room, where we combine playing with learning, and the babies are looked after in the next two rooms where we have cots and everything else they might need. We also have a nurse on duty. So shall we get started?"

"Thank you! I think I'll enjoy working here, Mrs Bell."

"Please call me Nora; we don't stand on ceremony here."

The morning went by very quickly. June enjoyed working with the children, and Amanda seemed happy mixing with them.

"Thank you, Nora."

"I'll see you tomorrow then, June."

"You certainly will. Bye!"

Lisa was waiting for her at the coffee shop.

"Tell me all. How did it go?

"Perfect! You know, I really enjoyed it."

"Good; and how was Tim this morning."

"Not as bad as he has been. He seems to be going from being angry to being indifferent."

"One extreme to another, is that it?

"June, I guess he was like that all over the weekend. Not one angry word; as a matter of fact, no words at all!"

"You should tell him, June. Try and make him understand his daddy was ill; after all, alcoholism is an illness."

"Yes, I know you are right; and I promise I'll talk to him tonight."

At four o'clock, Tim's school was finishing; and the dog was still waiting outside when Tim came out. The dog got up to move after him.

"What do you want, pooch? I told you I don't want you!"

But the dog had no intention of going anywhere else, only with him. Mr Madison, watching this, smiled to himself.

"That dog is going to stick like glue to that boy. I think I will go and see Mrs Smyth this evening. She might like to talk to a stranger, so to speak. I can't help being worried about that family."

Walking home, Tim kept telling the dog to go home but the dog was going nowhere.

"Why do you want to stay with me, pooch? Oh; ok then; come on: it's time we went home."

When he got home, he saw his mum was in the kitchen, cooking.

"There you are, Tim. Go wash up; dinner is almost ready. Up you get, Amanda: time to eat. Tim, it's your favourite: burgers and chips."

"I'm not hungry; I'm going to my room."

"Very well! I will not argue with you."

Later that evening, June put Amanda to bed. After reading her a story, she tucked her in.

"Night, sweetheart; go to sleep now, I have to go and check

on your brother."

"Good night, mummy."

Going into Tim's room, she was surprised to see the dog.

"I wondered where you were. I thought you did not want this dog, Tim."

"He won't leave. So, if he wants to be stupid and stay, I won't stop him; unless you want to get rid of him, same way you did dad."

"I did not send your dad away; he went himself."

"I don't believe you. I don't want to talk to you anymore."

"If that's what you want! Good night, Tim."

Downstairs, June started to tidy up. As she worked, she wondered what she was going to do about her son.

"Well God, I guess this is not the time to talk to him about his dad."

Sitting down, she was thinking of all that had happened in the last year.

"Where are you, David? Our son is hurting so much!"

At first she did not hear the knocking on the front door.

"Oh, who could this be?"

Opening the door, she was shocked to see Mr Madison standing there.

"Good evening, Mrs Smyth. I hope you don't mind. I just came to see if you were alright and perhaps it was foolish. I thought you might like someone to talk to, a stranger, more or less."

"No; I don't mind. Please come in. Sit down. Would you like tea or coffee, Mr Madison?"

"Coffee, please, and, since we are not in school now, I would like you to call me Tom."

"On one condition; you call me June."

Smiling, he said, "You have a good boy in Tim, but the change in him is hard to understand. What has your husband to say about it?"

Lowering her head, she said, "That is what's wrong with Tim; his dad left a year ago without a word. That's why he's changed; he adored him."

"So that's it! I'm sorry, June. Has he not been in touch at all?"

"No, I have tried to find him. I even hired a private detective; but to no avail. I guess he did not want to be found."

"Don't mind if I ask you this, but did anything happen to make him leave?"

"David, my husband, started drinking about two years before he left. I watched him change from a loving husband and father to a total stranger. I tried to get him to go and get help. I got all the information about AA meetings, and how they could help him; but he would not accept he had a problem. As far as he was concerned, there was nothing wrong. I myself went to a family support group, but, no matter what I did, he would not admit he was ill. As time went on, his drinking got worse. I started finding bottles of vodka and whiskey hidden around the house; and still he said there was nothing wrong; he could handle it. Then, the day before he left, I looked everywhere for bottles. Any I found went down the sink, I had to do something. Tim was getting older and I did not want him finding these bottles or thinking that alcohol for breakfast and tea was normal. Anyway, that night Tim was staying over in his friend's house and my friend, Lisa, took Amanda to stay with her. When David came home, the first thing he did was look for his bottles. When he could not find them, he went berserk, throwing and breaking things; shouting, 'where are they?' I told him I had poured them down the sink. He hit me a few times. He was like a mad man. I could not believe this was the same man I married. "

Suddenly they heard shouting from the stairs,

"No, no! You're lying. Dad would not do that to you."

Tim ran at her, hitting out at her in his anger.

Tom grabbed and held him.

"Tim, I'm so sorry. I never wanted you to find out like this."

Pulling away from Tom, he ran to his room, sobbing as though his heart would break. June ran after him.

"Tim, please!"

"Leave me alone!"

Coming down to the sitting room again, she said, "Why did he have to hear that?"

"Sit down, June. Would you like me to make you a coffee, or something?"

"No thanks, Tom. I'm fine."

"Tell me what the relationship between Tim and his dad was like."

"Oh; it's very special. I remember when he was born, David took him from the doctor's arms. 'Look June, we have a son; thank you, darling; thank you.'"

As she talked, Tom could picture what she was saying in his head.

"Hey, honey, I'm home. Where's my little man?"

"Please, David; keep it down. I just got him asleep."

"Laughing he would say, 'I won't wake him; I just want to see him.' 'David, come on your meal is ready.' 'Thanks honey; you know, when he gets a little older, he and I will go to football matches. Sure, I'm looking forward to it, watching him grow; playing with him; doing all the things with him my dad did with me. I had a happy childhood and that's what Tim is going to have.'"

"Tom, Mr Madison, are you listening?"

"Sorry I was picturing what you were telling me. Your husband must have loved Tim very much."

"Yes, he did. I think he always will. You know, when Tim was four his dad got him a train set, and, after the birthday party was over, he set up the train in the play room and the two of them would play for hours. They would spend so much time together; and the way they laughed all the time! The bond between them was very strong. But, not long after Amanda was born, he started to change, he had been promoted and he worked longer hours. Don't get me wrong: his love for his children was and, I hope, still is very, very strong."

She smiled sadly at Tom, saying, "Amanda was his princess and Tim was his main man, so I don't understand why he left us."

"June, speaking as a man, maybe he was afraid that, if he stayed, he would hurt you or even the children. Perhaps hitting you was a wakeup call."

"If that's so, why did he not stay? We could have worked it out together."

"Yes, but you don't know what was in his mind. Anyway, June, God is good. I'm sure that something good will come out of all this. Well, it's late. I better go. I've still got papers to grade."

"Thank you for listening."

"Happy to be of some help, even it's only listening. Good night, June."

"Goodnight, Tom. Thanks again."

After locking up, June went upstairs. Stopping at Tim's room, she went in. Tim's eyes were closed.

"Good," she thought. "He's asleep."

She went into her own room.

"That was not honest, pretending to be asleep; was it Tim?"

"Who said that? Who's there?"

"Don't get excited; it's only me."

"Pooch? I'm hearing things; dogs don't talk."

"They don't, but, then, I'm not just any dog. I'm magic."

"Shut up. There's no magic."

"There is; it's only that people have closed their minds to it. What do you think you are doing?"

"I'm getting out of here."

"To do what?"

"I'm going to find my dad."

"You're running away! What good is that going to do? You are only going to worry your mum."

"I don't care, I'm going."

"Fine! I won't stop you. I won't even bark; but I'm coming

with you."

"Why; and how come you're talking?"

"Someone has to look after you, and I already told you: by magic. By the way my name is Star, but, if you want to call me pooch, that's fine."

"Tim, what's keeping you? Please come down. No answer from your brother's room, Amanda my sweet! I better go up to him; he was so upset last night."

Opening the bedroom door, she discovered Tim was gone, as was his school bag; and the dog.

Sighing, she went back down to Amanda.

"Your brother's gone already. I guess he did not want to talk to me. Well, we'll meet him later at the school. Come on, we have to go, or I'll be late for work."

Mr Madison was checking the attendance book, and realised Tim Smyth was absent. Thinking back to the previous night, he felt sad for June Smyth and her family.

"I guess he was too upset to come to school. I hope things work out for that family. I have to admire the courage of Mrs Smyth, trying to keep trying to keep things going while her heart was breaking."

Turning away from the Smyth family, he got on with his own work.

After work, June and Amanda went shopping; then home for lunch. She felt like a robot doing things without thinking, her mind on Tim; hoping he was alright.

"Mum, phone ringing!"

"Oh sorry, darling; my mind was miles away."

"Hello, June; it's Lisa. What are you doing?"

"I'm just going to meet Tim from school," going on to tell her what had happened the night before, "and, Lisa, do you know what today is?"

"Yes, it's Tuesday."

"Tuesday, the third of February! It's a year since David left."

"June, I'm sorry; I did not think. Look, I'm not doing anything; so I'll meet you at the school."

"Great; thanks! See you then!"

At the school Lisa and June were waiting when the children started to come out.

"Lisa, I don't see Pooch; he normally waits at the gate for Tim. Since he came to us, he goes to school with him and waits all day for him to come out."

"Don't worry. Maybe he wandered off, like dogs do."

"Hello, Mrs Smyth."

"Hello, Billy; how are you?"

"Fine! Is Tim sick?"

"No; why do you ask?

"He was not in school; that's why. I thought he was sick."

"June, you're as white as a sheet."

"Here, take Amanda."

"Where are you going?"

" Tim must be in there. I'll see Mr Madison."

"Mr Madison, where's Tim?"

"He did not come in today. I thought you kept him home."

"No. I went to his room this morning; but he and his school bag were gone. I assumed he had left early because he did not want to talk to me."

"Now, don't panic; perhaps he just skipped school because he was still upset and angry. Come on; we'll go to your house; my car's outside."

"Lisa and Amanda are at the gates."

"Right; we will pick them up on the way."

Back at the house, there was still no sign of Tim.

"O God, Lisa, what am I going to do?"

"First things first! Have you any idea where he might have gone, like would he have a favourite place he would go to if he was upset or wanted to be alone?"

"I'm not sure. I know he and his dad used to spend a lot of time in the park; but a favourite place? Wait a minute! I remember Tim once told me that he and his dad hung around at a big tree near the pond. As a matter of fact, they wrote their names on it. They would spend hours there."

"Right," said Mr Madison; "I'll drive there. June, you stay here with Amanda. You must try and keep calm. No point in upsetting the little one. Lisa, you come with me; we can split up and search more ground that way, just in case he's not at the pond. June, you have my mobile number. Ring if he comes back."

At the park they went to the pond.

"There are a lot of trees here, Mr Madison."

"Yes there are. By the way, Lisa, call me Tom. Look; you start that side. I'll do this side. If you find anything, call me; and we'll go from there."

"Right, Tom; will do."

A short time later, Lisa heard Tom calling her.

"What is it?"

"This is the tree. Look, their names are here."

Moving around the tree, Lisa's foot hit something, pushing the loose twigs out of the way, she bent down to see what it was.

"Look, Tom! It's Tim's bag – but no Tim! He can't be far away. Let's keep searching."

After an hour, they had covered the whole park.

"Well, he's not here! He can't be far away, Tom. At least, I hope not."

"Come on, Lisa. Let's get back in the car. We can drive around the streets. Are you married, Lisa."

"No, almost! He left me at the altar."

"Oh! I'm sorry."

"Don't be: it was a long time ago."

"Tom, I know you are trying to get my mind off Tim. Do you think Tim will come home?"

"Yes; but 'when' is the question. The streets can be a dangerous place for a little boy."

In the meantime, Tim was trudging the streets with Pooch at his side. Looking around, he spotted Tom's car. Grabbing Pooch, he ran into a side street and hid until the car had passed.

"Hey kid, what you doing? You got any money?"

"I'm not doing anything; and I don't have any money."

"Come here, kid; empty your pockets."

Tim was frightened. Looking around, he fell over a box.

As the man advanced, Tim called Pooch for help. The man laughed as Pooch stood in front of Tim.

"You think I'm afraid of that mutt?"

But then he went very quiet.

Tim looked up to see what had happened. The man's face was white; and he looked scared; and there was Pooch seeming to grow, but it was that the light that shone around him was awesome.

The man turned and ran, and then the light was gone and Pooch was himself again.

"Pooch, how did you do that?"

"Magic! Now do you understand why you should be at home with your mum and sister, where you would be safe?"

"I know, pooch; but I still want to find my dad, I miss him so much."

"Your mum is hurting too, you know. But tell you what I will do! I'll take you to see your dad, if you go home after you see him, and tell your mum how sorry you are."

"She drove him away."

"No, she did not; and, Tim, deep down you know that. Now, before I do this, I must tell you; you will see him and hear him but he will not be able to see you."

"How will that happen? Oh, I know! Magic!"

"Now, hold on to me and don't let go."

It seemed to Tim that they had not moved, but here they were in a room with about ten people.

"Where are we, pooch?"

"We are at an AA meeting."

"What's an AA meeting?"

"It's a place where people come for help. They come to talk about their problem; and that is that they drink far too much. In other words, drink has taken over their lives, and caused a lot of unhappiness in their families."

"You're telling me that my dad is a drunk."

"I'm telling you your dad is sick. It's a disease like any other."

"Oh! I see! Look, there's dad. He's standing up. Is he going to talk?"

"Yes, and you should listen."

"Hello, everyone! My name is David Smyth, and I am an alcoholic. A year ago in a drunken rage I struck my wife. When I woke up next morning, I realised what I had done. It was a wake-up call for me. I love my family very much, and the thought that I could hurt my wife like that frightened me. So I left. Now I think I can go back, and know I will never touch a drink again. I only hope they can forgive me and take me back. One other thing; I'd like to say to anyone here who has just started coming to these meetings: stick with it; never give up, and, in the end, it will be worth it.

Thank you."

Then Tim and Pooch were back on the street.

"Now I know mum was telling the truth. I'm going home now."

"Great! Now you're talking!"

When they got to the house, Tim was afraid to go in.

"It's alright. She'll be happy to see you. Hurry; they are just going to call the police!"

Going in, Tim got a shock to see his mum's tear-stained face. Lisa was comforting his little sister; and Mr Madison had the phone in his hand.

"Mum, I am sorry."

"Tim, oh my god I was so worried, where were you?

"I was trying to find dad. Mum, please don't be angry; I am really sorry."

"Please, Tim, don't ever do that to me again."

"I promise. And, mum, dad is coming home!"

The three adults looked at him and then at each other.

"How do you know that?"

"I know."

"Tim, don't build your hopes up; we have not even heard

from your dad."

Bending down he put his arms around Pooch,

"I just know."

"I believe you. But now you need a bath and something to eat; you must be hungry."

"Yes, mum."

In the bathroom, Tim said to Pooch, "No point in telling them about you; they would not believe it."

"No, they would not; although Mr Madison might; he knows there is something different about me."

Downstairs, Lisa said to June,

"We'll go now, and let you get on with it."

"Yes, thank you both; I don't know what I would have done without you."

"No thanks needed."

Amanda was dancing around clapping her hands:

"Tim home; Tim home!"

Sweeping her into her arms June said, "Yes, darling, your brother is home. Well goodnight, June. Goodnight, and thank you."

On the drive home, Tom said, "I think they are going to be alright now, Lisa."

"I know they are; thank God."

At Lisa's door, Tom said to her, "Will you come out to dinner with me tomorrow night, please?"

"I'd like that, Tom. Until then, good night; drive safely."

After he had eaten, June said to Tim: "I was so worried about you. I did not know what to think."

"I know, mum, I was stupid to run away. I should have listened to you."

"You're home safe now; and that's all that matters."

"Yes, mum; and Pooch looked after me. He would not leave me, even though …"

"Yes, love, he is special. Now, time for bed; you must be tired."

"Goodnight mum," Amanda hugging them both.

Next morning, Tim was up before his mum called him.

"Pooch, why do I get the feeling you're going to leave soon?"

"My job with you is done. Another child needs a touch of magic, but I won't go until tonight. In five minutes someone else will want to talk to you."

Looking at Pooch, it dawned on Tim: "It's dad; he's coming home." Running down the stairs, he shouted, "Mum …"

"One moment, Tim, there's a knock at the door."

Opening the door, she was stunned to see David standing there.

"Hello, love. May I come in?"

"Yes, of course!"

When he walked in, Tim threw his arms around him, and Amanda pulled at his jacket.

Looking at June, he said, "Can you guys ever forgive me?

"Are you home for good?"

"If you will have me."

Taking her in his arms, he said, "I'm so sorry for everything. I have missed you and the children so much. But I wanted to get better before I came home."

Kissing him, she said, "We can talk later. Right now, the children have to eat breakfast."

That evening, Tim said, "When are you going, Pooch?

"I have something to do first; then I'll come back to say goodbye."

With that Pooch vanished. "Magic!" said Tim.

Tom Madison sat in his living room. Suddenly, Pooch was there.

"Hey where did you come from?"

"I think you know, Tom; a dog helped you when you were little."

Staring at Pooch, "Of course I remember. I knew there was something about you."

"Tom, you said back then that you wanted to be a teacher."

"Yes, and I am."

"True, but you wanted to teach in countries where there are no schools; and that's where you are needed."

"I have been thinking about that a lot lately."

"You will do it before the year's out and you will have a partner with you."

"Who?"

"Lisa!"

Back in Tim's room, Pooch said goodbye.

"I wish you would stay."

"I can't; but you and your family are going to be alright now."

"Why do you have to go?"

"Because someone else needs me, a little girl called Megan; but I want you to remember there is magic in this world, in a kind word, a smile, a helping hand to someone who needs it, in the sky, the sun, the way the stars come out at night, and if you call for help there is someone up there listening. Never forget."

"I understand. This little girl, Megan, she needs a touch of magic?"

"Yes, Tim, a touch of magic! I must go now. Goodbye Tim."

"Goodbye, Pooch. I'll never forget you."

O'Connor, Seán

Macker

It was three o'clock on a Friday afternoon that Jack called me – at my office. That was the first thing that surprised me: where on earth had he got my office number? The voice was the same.

"Hi ya, Tony! How are things with you?"

"Jeez Jack, long time no see. How has life been treating you?"

"Fine, Tony, Fine. Listen, I'll be killed. Our class re-union is tomorrow afternoon and you must be there. It's the twenty first so you must come down. I'll pick you up at the train and you can stay at my place."

"I don't know Jack. It's fierce short notice."

Muriel persuaded me to go, so I would go, down to see all the hopeful eighteen year olds I had left all those years ago. How would they be? How would they look? How did I look? June 1966 we were full of hope, full of the aggressive love of youth going out to conquer the world, our love, our youth, our 1966.

There was a certain degree of apprehensiveness about me the next morning as I dressed. Those friends of my school days – they were now almost strangers – even Jack. I hadn't seen him in, how long, five, six years? The rest for twenty!

Jack was now in charge of what was once his father's

building firm. He had also married and was now living in the old house, a beautiful spacious one, in Ballincollig, with large manicured gardens running down to the river. We had hunted the semi-wild cats over that and adjoining gardens as kids, putting them to swift flight with pellet guns. And in later years, we would skip last class on a Wednesday, and borrow Jack's mother's car for a fast drive to Kinsale or Crosshaven. Fifteen minutes was our record – in the Ford Escort, from the speed limit sign on the Airport road to the one outside Kinsale. One night coming back the car aquaplaned: I thought we were done for. I pretended to enjoy it, though inwardly I was shaking. I thought Jack was a bit frightened too, though he didn't say anything either.

On the journey to Cork, I thought back on our teen years, and it struck me how good it might have been if only we could have had the experience of age on our young shoulders. But, of course we could not. However, I suppose we did our best and some of the times were good. There were nights in Crosshaven and Fountainstown: they were good crack, trying to impress the girls who always acted unimpressionable. Perhaps we were a bit silly, but still, the exuberance of youth is a great thing, and its energy makes up for its lack of experience.

I told Fiona some of the better stories on the way down: I didn't tell her about how insecure we all felt sometimes. Considering all, I suppose we didn't do so badly – after all this was still the sixties; and the Catholic Church was still very much in charge. And yet, the country, even then, was beginning to drag itself into modern times. Sex was still a sin, of course, even if a little less so, and the grip of the clergy had begun to slip a little. Now I sometimes worry a little about how the world is heading: I suppose in a way we helped to create it. That is the worst aspect.

The hotel foyer was buzzing when we entered. I had called to Jack's and found everything almost exactly as I had remembered it, almost as if everything had been left in a time warp during the years I was away. I sat for tea exactly where I had often sat as a child, looking out over the beautiful gardens: even the little gate was still there at the bottom. For some reason I was glad about that. Jack's wife served the tea and I felt immediately at home, immediately welcome – almost as if I had never left.

At five we went to the school. We visited the old play yard and went upstairs to the old senior school. I really didn't like it any more than I did as a pupil: if anything it was even more dismal. It was deserted; and the ghosts of the teachers, some now dead, seemed to patrol the corridors. Then to the new school, built across the road on the playing fields where we used to play rugby. The fields were now covered by a large, modern-designed school, and I thought, what a shame to build over our playing fields like that. This is where we first kicked the oval ball at age seven and had cried when we got kicked ourselves. It was where we learned about life – winning, losing and getting hurt. It was also where we laughed and had fun. Now it was gone, so what the hell! Time won't stand still to suit me. Jack seemed to read my thoughts.

"Shame to have the fields gone, Tony," he said. "The old school was getting too small and its age was against it also."

"I guess so," I replied not fully convinced. "Anyway, why

should I bloody care?"

But yet, I suppose I must have. There were some good days there, as well as the bad and the mediocre.

In the new school, they were all gathered about, talking and laughing, the early, impressing, stage being enacted. A temporary bar had been set up, and whiskey and beer were being dispensed into paper cups. I was surprised at the number of guys I remembered, and how many I had forgotten. There was Danny McCarthy the suave, now a senior Public Official, Counsellor Peter Maguire, publican Philip Moran, Insurance Broker Matty Curran, Father Sean Donegan, Quantity Surveyor James Madigan, Company Director Paddy Donavan, Kevin Cregan and of course the class captain, Michael Mellott.

There was also my old friend Bob Kelly, now a dentist, and Simon Cooke, who is a professional photographer. There wasn't Otto Kellett, who lives abroad, or Peadar Greene, who is dead, or Seamus Cullen, who is also.

And there wasn't Alexander McCarthy, – Macker. Macker hadn't arrived yet. At first the story about him was funny, especially when everybody had had a few jars. And yet, how can a story of anguish and degradation be funny? How can a story of wasted intelligence and a wasted life be told to amuse: because I quickly realised that there was really nothing funny about the story.

Macker had been my friend since second class. He had pushed me into study and into rugby, even if I didn't shine at either. Macker was a big boy, and he was funny and popular and sincere, and he took the time to encourage a less than confident seven year old.

But he couldn't control the demon drink; and now it had him in the gutter. He had a promising career as a journalist, lost forever because he couldn't control his drinking. I found this to be extremely sad, and even more so the thought that there was nothing that anybody could do for him. We had grown together, studied together and played together. Yet in the years since I had last seen Macker, he had worked for a time, loved, married (for a time) and then slipped backwards into the morass of alcoholism, till now he had nothing, was nothing. And their well-meaning words, the new suit, the collection made for him after dinner, really meant nothing, because tomorrow he would sell the suit and spend the money on a bottle and then he is back to where he has been for a long time – in the gutter.

And he and I sat in the bar, and Macker told me his story. We drank steadily and he looked intently into my face and told me: how he had gone to America in '67 and worked in Los Angeles as a junior reporter. In 1969 he had joined the army as a way, he thought, to get his citizenship. And then he found himself in Vietnam and the bombing and the shooting and the cruelty. It made a deep impression on his sensitive, intelligent spirit. And then he was shot – once in the stomach and once in the side of the head.

Then he was shipped home – to Ireland, to work in the *Cork Examiner*. But he couldn't cope with it. He couldn't tame the turmoil in his head and the constant buzzing around and around, day after day, with one trivial story after another trivial story, until he thought his brain was going to burst.

And: there were missed days and missed headlines. One day they sent a messenger to his lodgings. Macker had been dreaming about Vietnam and thought the messenger was from the Vietcong.

After that they fired him: the messenger ended up in hospital.

The next day I went to the 'Orchard' with my Old Man. John Hedigan, who was our outhalf at Pres, was there, at the bar, with his Old Man.

"Jeez John," I said to him, "That was a terrible story Macker was telling me last night about himself. He certainly has been through the mill."

"Don't mind him, Tony. That never happened. He's fecking mad. He's for the fecking birds. Don't mind him."

I thought, how dreadful that was; and I remembered also meeting Peter Sherbert the night before, who had just drunk his family bakery out of business. He was drunk too, and wanted to tell me his story. But I didn't feel like listening to him, and I had said "You'll be OK, Peter," and walked on. I don't know why I didn't stop and listen, even for a while. Imagine to imagine you were shot in Vietnam. Imagine to drink your family business into ruin. Imagine what lies between your emergence from the womb and your lowering into the grave.

I left Macker when the call came for the photograph. He stayed in the bar. He isn't even in the picture of the night. As far as history is concerned, he isn't there. The story of his life – missing the photo-call!

"And sometimes to return is to find you've never left. And the ghosts of the present are the same ones you've left behind."

Alexander McCarthy died from lung cancer at the Mercy Hospital, Cork. He was forty one years old. May he rest in peace!

This is based on a true story, but names and some details have been changed.

O'Connor, Sean

Pol Gorm

Sitting here on the edge of the world,
Watching the gulls, listening to the sea;
On the bay a schooner with sails unfurled;
Here I find peace and serenity.

Pol Gorm remembered from my youth.
Nostalgia, now it is past and gone!
Looking back, it seems so long ago:
The sea and the rocks, the sky and the sun.

I like the memory of the rolling waves,
Like a savage animal which lunges to devour,
Surf hissing, frothing at the mouth,
Through rocks and over the pebbled shore.

We passed here for a fleeting moment,
On our way through life, two friends and I,
And each coming was a new love,
A new sea and a new sky.

And we would walk along the shore,
Together, as only true friends can be,
Relaxed together – nothing to prove;
Just the rocks and the noise of the sea.

Finally, with rustling evening trees,
And the wind now turning cold,
We would turn and take our leave,
To return to a mundane world.

Nostalgia is: missing that which went before,
Remembering places, fond faces; and we
Shed a tear for what we have no more:
It is we have changed, not sky and sea.

> This is taken from Seán's collection of poems: *Taking a Risk with Love*, available from Amazon.

O'Connor, Seán

On Infinity in the World

I was halfway up Sliabh-na-mBan and the sun was shining across the valley spread out beneath me. And then it just struck me that I was here on the side of a mountain while the rest of the world went about its business down below.

To me at the time, this was a rather profound thought. It struck me also that I was here at a particular point of time that never was before and never would be again, for we formulate our own history, second by second, minute by minute, on to Eternity. And I wonder where I was before I was and where will I be after I am. That is the wonder of Eternity – its relevance with Time.

Over the last thirty years or so, the Metaphysicist, Stephen Hawking, has made a number of important contributions to the science of Cosmology – which is the study of the origin and nature of the Universe. One of his contributions, his "black holes" theory, stating that black holes in the Universe can emit radiation, has opened up a complete new way of looking at the origin of the Universe, and shows that it is possible to combine Einstein's Theory of Relativity, which expresses things at a very large, cosmic level, with Quantum Theory, which is used to describe the very small, at the level of atoms.

And where does this tie in with the Christian Bible? Quantum Gravity can be described as the field of theoretical physics which attempts to develop Scientific Models that unify Quantum with General Relativity. If we describe the beginning of our world, it is now believed that it all began with the smallest possible of molecules (one single molecule - Singularity), containing infinite energy, which expanded to create infinite galaxies in (infinite) outer space. This is an astounding concept – the creation of matter and anti-matter in almost equal proportions. So, can we tie up Faith and Science and how they correspond (interact?) with each other? If we take the Bible's explanation of the beginning of our world in the Book of Genesis, it presents us with a simple explanation of the creation of everything – God, the all powerful, infinite Being.

Science, on the other hand provides a different explanation. According to a scientific hypothesis, the Universe began about fifteen billion years ago with the Big Bang, when a singularity expanded spontaneously. No one knows why, of course. But the Universe is still expanding and will continue to do so for another few billion years, when it will reach a point when the expansion will stop. Again, no one knows why. One theory suggests that it will then dissipate to nothing, so that all activity will cease and all its energy will bubble away. Other theorists suggest that everything will start to run in reverse, to squash itself again into a singularity.

And which Bible should we use? It actually does not matter that much. For four hundred years following on from the Reformation, the different branches of Christianity went their own separate ways; and suspected each others' translations of the Bible as been in some way manipulated in the interests of doctrinal presuppositions. It would have to be admitted that these suspicions were not always without foundation. Translation from the original language of writing is an essential priority, as much of the meaning can be lost through translation. There is now large agreement on this between the various Denominations.

Having said that, however, it must be said that the Bible is not a scientific document, but rather a series of books written over a long number of years and whose emphasis was to tell the story of creation and the development of the human race to (largely) uneducated people. The ancient Jews had no precisely-defined Canon of Scriptures: many of the Old Testament books were written in Hebrew or Aramaic and were fairly widely circulated outside Palestine in a Greek translation. The first book of the Old Testament is the First Book of Moses, commonly called Genesis; and this Book begins with a description of the beginning or our world. The aim of the narrative is not really to present a scientific picture but to teach religious truth, especially the dependence of all creation on God; and mans' dependence on this Being we call God for everything he requires. And yet, there is nothing in the early chapters of Genesis that commits to any particular scientific view of the origins of the world or man, or that would exclude the evolution hypothesis. Indeed, as we have already noted, the Metaphysical theory, with a little modification, could fit in nicely.

Then, we might ask – just what is Infinity, for that is what we speak about when describing our Galaxy and the millions of Galaxies outside of ours. Well! We might just as well try to analyse Joxer's question in O Casey's "Juno and the Paycock" – "What is the stars, what is the stars?" It is actually a good question: it can take hundreds of light years for the light of some of the stars that we know about to reach earth, travelling at the unimaginable speed of 299,792,458 metres per second, or, in Imperial Units 186,282 miles per second. A light year is the distance that light will travel in one year and equals 9.46053×10^{12} kilometres or 5,880,000,000,000 miles. It can take many, many of these light years for the light of a star to reach earth – how large is Infinity, you might rightly ask, or how small?

Actually, there are two concepts of Infinity, one for mathematics and one for philosophy. Potential Infinity, which is the infinity of a process that never stops, encompasses mathematical definitions, something like 2, 4, 6, 8 and so on for ever and ever and Actual Infinity, which is supposed to be static and completed, so that it can be thought of as an object, something like all the Galaxies out there up in the sky.

The Cybernetic philosophy, which is the branch of science concerned with control systems and comparisons between mad-made and biological systems, readily embraces the concept of Potential Infinity: in fact it is hard to see how we can avoid it. We may say that a process ends when it reaches a certain stage. In a particular case, we can define the end stage so that it never takes place. This is an abstraction: we have abstracted from the practical impossibility to run any real process indefinitely. In this abstraction, no matter how long we run a process, we can do or observe the next step. In other words, where we have Time or Movement, we cannot really have Infinity. This is why Infinity is called "potential." At every specific stage, the process involves no more than a finite reality: it is not infinite, only potentially.

For actual infinity we have no place in our system of concepts. We cannot imagine anything that would qualify as actual infinity, because neither we, nor our evolutionary predecessors ever had anything like that in experience. When we try to imagine anything infinite – e.g. Infinite Time, we actually imagine a process moving from point to point without any end in sight. This is potential, not actual infinity.

If, on the other hand, we admit to the possibility of say, Infinite Distance, it is reasonable that we should accept also the possibility of Infinite Time. If we admit to an Infinite Cause to the Universal happenings we call our World, it will eventually lead us back to the point of "The Beginning" – material, spiritual or a combination of both.

And yet, if what we perceive is a movement of distance or time from a "beginning" to the present moment, we in fact do not have infinity at all, but a process moving from point to point – i.e. from there to here and possibly moving on from here. But if we do admit to the possibility of Infinite Time and Space, then we have to wonder about the Cause, infinite or otherwise – God. Infinity in historical terms would suggest infinity henceforth also: so at least the One we call God would appear to possess the possibility of an infinite future, just as we humans are promised. Yet, we are all biologically created at a specific time and the question over our heads is whether we are entitled to share an infinite future or whether we are merely a set of chemical reactions and electrical impulses that begin for us at the moment of our conception and finish when we die. The question is who created (us) computers and why?

When one thinks about it, the only impression we can have of God are his creations: and what are they and how do they work? They work through the laws of the Universe – the very small to the very big. An atom is pretty small – it cannot be seen through an ordinary microscope. Protons and neutrons and circulating electrons are smaller again. There is, maybe, no such thing as the smallest thing for everything is made up of a number of other things. Some Scientists call this the "God Particle." And then there is a *photon*, which is mass-less. A *hadron* is an elementary particle and is made up of *quarks*. The largest thing in the Universe is the *Sloan Great Wall* a super *Cluster* 1.37 light years in width. The entire known Universe is approximately 47 billion light years. The left-over radiation from the original Big Bang comes to us from everywhere in space and has taken the entire age of the Universe to reach us.

The speed of light (in a vacuum) is said to be 186,282 miles per second. Photons can travel at this speed because they have no mass. This is a constant set down at the time of the Big Bang where everything started. In a Black Hole, matter is so dense that the laws of regular physics just break down. A Black Hole can be any size – what determines its size is the amount of matter it sucks in.

And, what is the thing we call "mind?" It's our ego, our conscious "I," and it is a mystery, this "self," which is the deep, real us, that which defines each of us. We may ask whether it is the same as our brains, or whether perhaps our brains are just electrical impulses and nothing else: perhaps it as Stephen Hawking asks,

"............. Even if there is only one possible Unified Theory, it is just a set of rules and equations. What is it that breaths fire into the equations and makes a Universe for us to describe?"

What Hawking is trying to describe, in the way of the Atheist, is what believers call God. God is really the only Infinity, the Alpha and the Omega.

And what is the significance of this? It is this: if we do not have Infinity we do not have God as we know Him, for our perception of God is based on Him being infinite. This being the case, we could not ourselves claim to be infinite henceforth, because we depend on God being infinite to have any claim towards infinity for ourselves. If the One we call God is not infinite, then neither by implication or association can we be.

Dublin 2009: I gave this as a speech at *Toastmasters* for my advanced programme. Nobody – surprise, surprise – understood what I was talking about. My *Evaluator* thought it sounded great but that she hadn't a clue what I was talking about – come to think of it, neither did I.   Seán.

Editor's comment: Clareville Centre hosts a weekly Socrates Café, where questions of life are discussed. We sit around a large table. First, we have breakfast, and then a discussion is opened. All views and questions are welcomed and respected, whether simple or erudite. Contributions are usually brief, and all who wish are enabled to take part in the discussion.

Krunchie.

O'Doherty, Betty

Happy Days

Chapter 1

O how I wish to be young again!

Those were such happy days, especially in the Summer time. I loved going to the bog with the dinners and teas to my dad – and our good neighbours, who gathered together to save the turf for the winter fires.

As you may know, everything was cooked on that open fire in the kitchen. How well i remember the fine big cake mother baked in the oven (a heavy black pot with a lid) on that fire. Well, too, I remember the threshing of corn, when, again, our good neighbours came to help. A great big meal was prepared for them with plenty to drink to keep them in good spirits, and there was a song and a dance that night.

Another great day to remember was the bringing home of the hay. A fine meal of bacon and cabbage was cooked for all that helped. When the day's work was over, dad would take up his fishing rod, and off he went to the local lake.

On the lake we had our boat. We came home with lovely fresh fish for the dinner the next day. We had all our own vegetables and potatoes, so everything was really fresh. We had hens, ducks, geese, turkeys and pigs; so there was always plenty of activity around the house.

I remember a lovely dog-house we had for the dog. My dad

made it. He could make anything. He had this big box of tools. He also soled shoes for us around the winter and mother knitted our jumpers.

Chapter 2

I have lovely memories of my First Holy Communion and Confirmation. The church was two miles from home and we travelled there by horse and trap. On Sunday evening we visited grandmother and grandfather.

It's well i remember the big gramophone; and my favourite record was the *Red River Valley*.

I have heard it sung by *Foster and Allen* quite recently, so it must be making a comeback.

Grandfather was a lovely singer, and he went everywhere whistling a tune. Uncle John played the fiddle and mother played the accordion. Ours was a truly musical house.

At Christmas, my parents gave a big party which was called a spree. The boys and girls would all gather in the house and dance and sing until the small hours with plenty of refreshments laid on and drink galore.

Then, on St Stephens's Day, we all dressed up like boys, and took our musical instruments with us and sang and danced at every house we visited. We were the Wren boys. The neighbours were very generous and we divided the money among ourselves.

Of course Santa came, not in a big way like now. Nonetheless all was excitement on Christmas Eve: with the chimney being cleared for his arrival, cake on the table, and stocking hanging on the crook for him to fill. The magic and mystery of it all was fantastic.

Another big surprise was the parcel from America, with lovely smart dresses and jewellery. The local dressmaker did the needful if it were necessary. Also the Christmas box from the local shop! Plenty of goodies!

Chapter 3

Tea was in short supply in my youth, as those were war years. So coffee and cocoa were on the menu.

Luckily, we had our own butter which we made each week. It was a very important chore and you wore a white coat and hat and all dishes had to be spotlessly clean.

The travelling shop came around the country once per week, and he sold everything you needed from his van. The weekly paper was purchased on Sunday after mass.

A lot of news changed hands on Sunday mornings after mass – on the Chapel Cross, as they called it.

Old folk loved to get the news of the goings-on of the young people; so they made a point of leaning over half the door so you couldn't get past without them seeing you. We often ran over ditches and holes to avoid them.

And, of course, the fortune-teller called selling lace, clothes-pegs and bits and pieces. The men-folk mended leaking kettles and pots. The neighbours were very kind to the travelling people. They always put down their tent on the same place on the roadside.

Funerals were well-attended and the offerings were laid on a table in front of the altar. The Parish Priest got the money for himself.

I remember when someone died in the home, the neighbours all gathered and prayed for the night for the deceased. Refreshments were laid on.

Considering there were no daily papers around the area, it's amazing how people from neighbouring parishes heard about deaths. It was all done by word of mouth.

We were all pioneers in our youth and I remember my first big day out. Bundoran was the venue and it was a perfect day.

Chapter 4

There was no Christmas tree in our country at the time, as we had no electric light. It was a tallow lamp that we used back then, which burned oil and had a round glowing globe which I cleaned every night.

A bigger version of the lamp was to be found out in the outhouses.

At Christmas night, lightened red candles were placed in every window – glowing red. Out in the winter nights, they were a welcoming sight.

I remember the excitement that surrounded the arrival of our first radio, which was battery operated. It worked like magic, and all were in awe of it.

Neighbours gathered in our house of an evening – playing cards and storytelling. In those long winter nights, tales of haunted houses, ghosts and banshees crying for the dead and dying, left an eerie feeling.

I was also scared by an old man who used to come to our house to kill a pig every year. He frightened the living life out of me. Needless to say I hated to see the pig being killed. I always disappeared at that time.

It took days after to finish preparing the bacon and ham for the winter.

In summer chickens were killed for dinner, and at Christmas a goose.

We had our own ducks on the river at the bottom of the garden. It was my job to get them home in the evening, and, indeed, it was often quite difficult. They laid big green eggs, and dad had one for breakfast each morning. He also had porridge, as we ground our own meal. The mill was situated about two miles from our own house.

Chapter 5

Spring time in the country was glorious. Each day began with the sound of birds chirping in the trees at sunrise.

My dad would set off, with two horses pulling the plough, to ready the winter bare fields for the spring planting. From the kitchen window I could see not only my dad as he followed the horses, which I loved, across the fields, but also the beautiful flower beds by which the farm house was surrounded.

The beds were sprinkled with the red and yellow of the tulips and daffodils clear to be seen against the whitewashed wall. I cared for the flowers, and, in that same flowerbed, was born a love of flowers which survives to the present day.

There, too, were gooseberry bushes and apple trees, from whose juicy fruit mother made lovely tarts.

After school, we would take buckets of water from a spring-well nearby. The water was ice cold and crystal clear. The well was shaded from the afternoon's sun and it never went dry. Springtime, too, saw the arrival of new-born lambs and calves, which made extra work on the farm. Young chicks and turkeys arrived, and they had to be guarded against the eye of the hawk overhead.

My Birthday was in February, and I got a new dress and shoes which I kept for Summer. The season of Lent was next and, of course, we had to give up sweets, and the money we saved went into a box for the black babies. There were no Easter Eggs in the shops in those days.

Yes! It was wonderful to grow up in the country-side – surrounded by an endless carpet of green fields and rolling hills interspersed with fine old walls, great for climbing.

Even school, too, was great, with all the friends from far and near that we got to know.

Every day back then, each of us brought turf for the schoolroom fire. It was always warm right around the winter. We had a school-mistress and school-master, who were brother and sister; and they sure were cross! A long wooden cane sat on the master's desk and he could use it to the full. He often had reason to use it, as some of the pupils only did their homework on the way to school. Well, too, I remember the layout of the school room. Heavy wooden desks laid out in rows some high and some low. We all hated the high desks as the master could see all so clearly.

He was quite nice after school, as, if he met you in the shop, he would buy you sweets. We always had good fun on the way home from school at the end of each day.

Nearby there was a green grassy hill which we all thought perfect for rolling down from top to bottom. Nearer to home, we loved to pick juicy blueberries from the thorny bushes on a neighbour's land. But that farmer was occasionally cross, and always threatened that, if he ever caught us, he would sell us to a dealer who would make tin cans out of us.

Oerlemans, Hendrik Jan

A Sea Captain

To Whom It May Concern, 11/04/2012.

It all began on the 14th of April 1942 in Arnhem, Holland, and I had an average normal childhood until the 6th of May 1959, as the youngest son.

On that day (6 May 1959) I went to my first ship as a deckhand, and stayed at sea and loved it. I made it my home, never to live on land again. I made promotions throughout the years and climbed up to captain, in the Merchant Navy, on merit.

I got married in England in 1968, but still stayed at sea, as home and work was still at sea. The marriage ended unofficially in Dec 78. We officially divorced in 1980.

After saving some of the earned wages, I was able to put some money up for a partnership to buy a vessel in 1983, but, due to misfortunes, lost my investment.

I still stayed at sea, and climbed back up the ladder.

I still made the ships and sea my home and roamed the seven seas, until ill-fate struck me in 1995 (2nd of June), by suffering a stroke which left me somewhat paralyzed on the left side of the body.

Meanwhile, yet another venture of putting earned wages into a partnership by buying a vessel went wrong and, this time, left me broke financially; so, by the time I suffered the stroke and lost my job as captain, I was and still am out of financial resources, and have now no means of support.

Because I have no income anywhere in this world, and no home, and haven't lived ashore until recently, and have borrowed money from friends, who are now unable to advance more, as they have to look after themselves and their families, I turn to authorities here in Dublin to help me out, until I'll be able to return to sea or I die.

P.S.

I do have some family in Holland, but have not had contact with them. I also have two children in England, but I have very little communication with them. In between the sea voyages, I stayed with a friend, but he cannot look after me full-time; he has his own family to look after. I have made Ireland my home, for the last ten years. And, let's face it, Ireland is a great country, and the people are great, and, believe you me, I have met a lot of different people all over the world in thirty six years at sea.

Oerlemans, Hendrik Jan

An Interview with Captain Henk

> This is an account by a student of Dublin Institute of Technology, on placement in Clareville Day Centre, of an interview with Hendrik.

Henk grew up in The Netherlands in a city called Arnhem. Arnhem is bigger than Amsterdam, with over 20,000 Irish people living over there now.

In World War II, during Operation Market Garden (September 1944), the British 1st Airborne Division and the Polish 1st Independent Parachute Brigade were given the task of securing the bridge at Arnhem. This was a fierce battle. The Dutch Army destroyed the first bridge when the Germans invaded the Netherlands in 1940. The second bridge was destroyed by the US Army Air Forces shortly after the 1944 battle.

Henk was the captain of a ship in The Netherlands. He became a captain the day that John Wayne died (11th June 1979). He became interested in this profession when his older brother would return from voyages and share his exciting and exotic stories with him.

"That's what I want to do," he said.

His older brother was swept off Cape Town Pier in South Africa soon after this, and drowned.

Henk's mother wouldn't give permission for him to go to

sea. At the time, he needed both of his parents' permission, as he was under 16 years' old. When He turned 16, he set off for sea. His mother thought she'd never see him again.

Henk experienced many adventures while he was at sea. His first trip only lasted 6 weeks. He wandered off from the rest of the crew in Sweden, and they continued on to Finland, leaving him behind. He had to wait until the following day, when the company had another ship that would bring him to Finland.

Because it was due to his own negligence that Henk was stranded in Sweden, the company wouldn't pay for accommodation for him that night. He had to spend the night in jail, and was treated like a criminal.

He was only 16 years' old at the time. This seems quite young, but school-leaving age in The Netherlands at the time was fourteen, so all of his former classmates were out working.

Henk's favourite place to visit at sea was New Orleans in America. He visited there when he was chief captain. He said he preferred it so much more to New York, because it was disgustingly dirty there, especially at the harbour.

Henk met his wife at a quay-side shop that looks after the sailors etc., on the dock. He walked into the shop and asked for some wine gums. She told him that she liked wine gums too and he did the gallant thing of buying her a packet too. And that is where it all began.

He didn't regret not being there when his children were growing up. He didn't see them take their first steps or say their first words, but he didn't mind because he was working, doing what he loved. He would write letters home to the family.

You would think that Henk would have missed his family from being away from them for so long, but he didn't. He was happy doing what he was doing; and there was never time to think about it.

If the captain saw you doing nothing, he would find something for you to do. This consisted of doing a lot of painting on board.

He always wanted to better himself, so he wanted to become a Chief Officer. Henk became interested in all things to do with navigation when he got sea sick all over a compass!

The test was in Amsterdam; and he had to demonstrate how to navigate the ship. He failed the first time around. The examiner said he'd never pass the test. This was a good incentive for Henk to work harder and pass. When he repeated the test, he passed it.

When he told his mother the good news, she couldn't believe him. He brought her onto the ship one day when he was chief captain. She was so proud of him in his new black uniform! She embarrassed him in front of all the crew that day:

"Just because you're a chief officer now, it doesn't mean I can't give you a smack!"

All of the crew heard and were laughing at Henk.

In 1995 Henk was eating Dutch bread at 7.45 am. He hadn't eaten it in years. He swallowed it but it wouldn't go down. He tried to wash it down with a swig of coffee, but it still wouldn't go down his oesophagus. He couldn't breathe at the time, and he damaged one brain cell. This cell controls the left side of the body and now he is paralysed on that side.

Henk got a hernia. This happens when an organ pushes through an opening in the muscle that holds it in place. This happened a few miles from the Danish coast. He lives in Ireland now because he visited it once and liked the people. He thought the girls were warm and friendly.

While he was away, he learned how to speak Italian, Spanish, Portuguese, German and English. He has yet to learn Gaeilge!

Porter, Mary

Old Finglas

I was born in Finglas Village, at 1 Chapel Lane, in 1934. I lived in a small cottage with my mother, father, and two older brothers. The house was very small, with just two rooms and an outside toilet. My grandparents lived next door to us, and there were only 5 little cottages in a row.

My mother was born in the house next door, and moved to a flat in Mayor Street when she got married to my father, who was from Spencer Dock. After they were married, a house next door to my grandparents became available. Subsequently they moved in. At this point, one of my brother's, Michael, had died when he was 6 months old, and my younger sister, Josephine, came along.

Finglas is a very different place now. We had no running water or heating. As the oldest girl in the home, it was my responsibility to gather sticks and kindling for the fire each evening after school; for my house and my grandparents'. It was also my responsibility to fill the buckets from the well.

I remember playing out in the fields with my friend, Jenny. We would often go to the Parochial House, and we would open the gate for Father Russell, when he was coming home. As a reward, Father Russell would tell us to go around the back of the Parochial House to get bread and jam off the housekeeper, Ms Neelan. This was a big treat for us.

When I was aged 6 years, we moved to Tolka Estate, (where

I live now).

I remember when we first moved to the house. When we arrived, I couldn't believe how big and bare the house was. We had very little furniture, just a table, four chairs and a dresser, in the room, besides the range. I remember the great excitement, as we, the children, had our own bedroom; but yet I was very sad that I was no longer near my friend Jenny or my grandparents.

My parents then went on and had my younger sister, Eileen, and brother, Edward.

I went to the Holy Faith School in Finglas; however in those days, education was not deemed important for a girl from a working class background.

We didn't have a lot of money, and both my parents worked. My father worked in England intermittently, so often my mother had to balance caring for us and still working out of the home. My mother worked as a cleaner in Cassidy's Shop and Madame Nora's in the city centre.

I remember that I always had shoes and clothes, as a neighbour who was "well to do" would give me her daughter's old clothes. My sister and I both had a doll each, which we cherished.

When I was 13 yrs old, I had to leave school to look after my younger brother, while my mother worked.

I started my first job when I was 14 years old, caring for children of a judge who lived locally. I looked after two children, and also completed housework. I was paid 6 shillings per week, which all went straight to my mother.

After this, I got a job in The Button factory with my friend, Mary, in Drumcondra, when I was 15 years. I remember being given a rope to tie my hair up as I had very long hair, and, on occasion, we were sent home to iron our smocks, as the manager thought they were creased. This involved us walking from Drumcondra to home and then back to work. At that time I thought I was earning loads of money: One pound and a half-crown. I gave my mother the pound and spent the half-crown on toffee.

Times were very tough, as the war was on, which affected Dublin a lot. We had a ration book, and I remember going to Merville Dairy to try to buy butter on the black market.

Aftermath

At age 16 years, I moved to Liverpool to find work. I was terrified leaving Ireland and going on the boat by myself. I had a cousin living in Liverpool – and managed to find her house. I got a job in Crawford Biscuit factory, and sent money home every week. I was able to keep some money for the odd trip to the pictures and a lipstick. I then registered with an employment agent and I got a job in Wales in The Sherbert Hotel in Snowdonia.

I moved to Wales, and I was so happy to meet a neighbour from Ireland that I knew. We shared a room as live-in kitchen maids. Snowdonia was a beautiful place, and I remember this as being one of my favourite times in my early life. While working there, Edmund Hilary and John Hunt were staying in the hotel after their expedition to

Mount Everest. It was my job to serve them and I also walked their dog each day. They were very friendly.

I left Wales and moved to Birmingham two years later, as my friend was moving back to Dublin, and I didn't want to stay there by myself. I then secured work as a barmaid in Birmingham.

Rickard, Maureen

A Dublin Life

I was born in 1926, the third child in the family. I had one older brother and an older sister. Then came a younger brother and sister. Here comes the sad era of my life. Mother died in 1933, the day she gave birth to twins, who sadly died a couple of months apart from each other.

I had to go on a tram to tell the two grandmothers the awful news; of course there were no phones or mobiles. There were very few cars, only doctors and priests and professionals had one. I loved going on the trams, always upstairs in the front seat, making out I was a driver. The train to Bray was very lovely, but whatever you do don't put your head out the window, or you would get steam and smut in your eyes. Coming into a station you would hear a choo-choo, nearly there, nearly there!

Dad was wonderful. He did not drink or smoke. He always made sure that we wanted for nothing, and we had a happy time. Life was simple: we went for walks, and we cycled to the seaside. In the summer we took a house for a month in either Rush, Skerries, or Portrane.

One summer, however, we went further afield; my aunt brought my sister and me to the farmhouse in Avoca. I noticed two haystacks in the small patch of land, right in front of the house. Of course I had to climb one but it was full of thistles and nettles. I was stung all over. I don't think I was anxious to climb haystacks after that.

During a thunder-storm one night my aunt jumped under her bed and told us to do the same. Every time the crash and boom started she would roll her eyes and shout "oh, oh, oh! Jesus Mary and Joseph, keep us safe." My little sister, bless her, was terrified.

I now realise we were lucky dad had a good job, being a civil servant, working from an office on O'Connell Street, which was very near our home.

To drown in a river must be terrible; the son of the gatekeeper of the Botanical Gardens pushed me into the river, which can be fast-flowing sometimes. My hair was long and rested on top of the water. My brother saved my life. He got a medal for saving my life and dad wore that medal with pride on the chain of the watch in his waistcoat.

My First Confession:

All the girls went into the reverend mother's room one by one and knelt by her knee. We told our three sins and said act of contrition and went outside and said three Hail Mary's.

On the actual day of the first confession, we went over to the church and, when my turn came, I just went in and did as I always did, just came out said my three Hail Mary's. You know the rest.

Some weeks later, I went to St. Peter's in Phibsborough. Nobody was around. Imagine my surprise, when I saw the priest sitting there reading a prayer book. He looked at me and said, "speak up child." How I mumbled through I don't know. I had not made my first confession at all.

I was the first to get married and leave the nest. My brother and sister followed shortly after, and, of course, by then my oldest sister was a nun in the USA. It was eighteen years before we saw her again.

After my mother died, Dad was at his wits' end, having to work and have us kids looked after. We had four sisters to mother and each of us helped out. His youngest sister was the only one married – with three children. We spent all our holidays and weekends with them. We were one big happy family.

Marriage:
I loved being a mother. Our house always seemed full of children, my five and their friends. We loved the summertime most of all, as we were able to be out and about.

Of course, the kids would argue about things, even a fly on the wall, but generally speaking they were very good. Two sisters who lived nearby knocked on my door one day and asked if 1 would take them in, as their parents were killed in a horrific car crash. Kathleen was with us for nearly a year and Ann for a further year.

Louis, my husband, was a driver to begin with, in the CIE, which was handy when the kids were young, because we availed of the free housing for families. After a few years he went to Dublin Corporation for the rest of his working life.

Kathleen entered the convent and was sent abroad. Sadly she died in her twenties. I was truly sad to hear that.

Ann got married to Tony and had six children and is living in

Galway, so I have not seen her for a long time, but I will never forget them.

My husband, Louis, was a follower of the GAA. He went to a lot of matches. I was mad about this, as on Sundays I liked to have the family together. I was thinking of how I could resolve this dilemma.

One Sunday after mass, I decided to take a day off. I took a bus out of town, had my lunch, went for a walk in the country and got home just after tea. My husband asked where I had been, as the kids were asking for me, "well that's what you do on a Sunday," I said. It happened again, and I did the same thing and, when 1 came back, my darling started to laugh and said "I get the message; in the future 1 will take you all with me."

The next big match was in Navan and off we set. He parked the car beside the big blank wall and we could not get out of the car because it was raining. Of course, he went to watch the match and took our son. Luke never went again. He was not impressed. I didn't win.

Granny's visit:

A country woman, she was a unique lady. She never smoked or drank alcohol and never went on a train or a plane. She looked after her husband, her children, and her home. When her husband died, she decided to do all of these things, she went on a plane to visit her daughter. After being on a plane, being on a train did not do at all, it was too slow.

Our house is on the main road, and Granny would sit for

ages looking at the traffic going up and down the road. She took a nap every afternoon for an hour or two. My husband was home, thank god. One Saturday afternoon, when the dog started barking like something was wrong, we rushed up to her room to find smoke and a terrible smell. Granny had fallen asleep with a cigarette and it burned through the bed clothes and mattress and had started to burn the carpet.

Louis opened the window and threw out the bed and clothes onto the front lawn. Granny was lucky she did not follow in the blanket.

We laugh about it now, but it was scary at the time.

My children were lucky to have a granny in the country and an auntie who had eight children of her own. Mine took it in turns to go on holidays. When my twins were about ten years old, they made friends with two little girls who just moved around the comer. Slowly but surely, they were in our home and became like family. Wherever we were going they came with us. If it was a birthday, we had a little party in the house. Their father was dead and mother worked long hours in a shop.

When they grew up and moved away, we lost touch for a little while. I was a guest at Mary's wedding. She has two children. They tell me I am the link they have to their childhood. Their mother had one sister who died very young and father had one brother (a priest) which meant they had no cousins, aunts or uncles. They were like family to me, and to this day I see them a couple of times a year.

Of course, one by one they left the nest and I missed them terribly. When my youngest left, I cried and cried and, when my husband passed away, I thought it was the end of the world. It took time for me to realise how lucky I was to have such a loving family, be positive and enjoy the rest of my life.

I've made some mistakes in my life, but the best thing I've ever done is join Clareville Centre. I could not praise the people who run it enough. They are wonderful from the top to the bottom. They are always helpful, cheerful and kind. I love them all very much.

Rickard, Maureen

Take Your Time

Take your time to be aware of your surroundings,
Before each little thing you do,
Whether eating or drinking or having fun,
Whatever the task that needs to be done,
Just take your time.

Take time to be aware of the beautiful
World God has made;
See and enjoy the lovely sky,
The colourful flowers and trees up so high:
Take your time.

Take time to help each person along the way;
Whether young or old or rich or poor,
God loves each one, and that love will endure.

I, my humble self, want to thank
All those wonderful people who help us
Each day in Clareville Centre,
As we go on our way.
With God's love and strength,
Each moment can be
An act of praise for eternity.

Rooney, Angela

Our Van

It was such a good friend and, like all good friends, it would never let you down. But today is a very sad day; I am sorry to say, our van has been stolen, the same van that has taken us around the country on so many lovely holidays.

We would pack our cases and hang up our coats and my dresses in the back of the van. We would also take our folding table and chairs and look forward to having picnics out in the open air. If the weather was bad, or if it was raining, we would set up the table in the van, where we enjoyed so many lovely meals. So you see, bad weather never really stopped us from enjoying our trips down the Country.

So, may I make this small request? Will you keep a look out for a blue Hiace Van, 88 D 10219, or maybe you would light a candle to St. Anthony, so that we might get it back soon.

Rooney, George

A Girl Called Susan

Susan was a very pretty, 22 year old, girl who was the daughter of Margaret and John Boyle, and lived in a small town in the west of Ireland.

Her father was a senior member of the town Council and her Mother was a well-known Member of the local Country Women's Association.

Susan lived all her life in this small town, until she met, and fell in love with, a Commercial Traveller who used to visit her town from time to time. He would ask her out for evening meals and present her with lovely roses and flowers.

As time went by, she became more involved with him. It was some weeks later that he disclosed he was married and that he was being transferred to Holland and would not see her again.

To put it mildly, it was the SHOCK of her life.

It was short time later she discovered that she was pregnant. She kept it a secret for some time, until one day her Mother noticed that she was putting on a lot of weight. It was then she sat down and told her mother the full story. If she had known what her reaction was going to be, I am not sure she would not have told her.

I know it was the 1950s, and times were very difficult, but she thinks she could have been more understanding. She knew how things were then, but it was not what she had expected from her own mother.

Mrs Boyle turned to face Susan.

"There is only one thing you can do," she said. "You will not be able to stop here in this town; you would bring too much shame on to the family. The best thing for you to do is go to Dublin to your brother John, who will meet you at the train station, and he will get you fixed up with some place to stay."

She can remember the day that she arrived in Dublin. It was a cold and bleak November day.

John met her at the station, and brought her to a nice guest house, but when the landlady saw that she was expecting, she said it would be better she found some other place to stay,

Her brother, john, could not give her any more help; so she went off on her own to try and find a bed-sitter. She must have tried about ten different places before she arrived at a house in Clontarf. The lady who opened the door took one look at her and said:

"Come in; you look worn out."

She explained to the lady of the house all her problems.

It was in that house her baby was born. It was then she had to face life, and all that goes with it. First of all, she had very little money, nor could she go and earn some: she had a baby to look after now.

Before long she found that she could not cope. It was then she decided to put her baby up for adoption.

About two weeks later, a lady from the Social Welfare came around and told her that she had a couple who wanted to adopt the baby, and that they would be here tomorrow at 12 o'clock, and it might be better if she was not here when they arrived, as it was not the best idea for the mother of the baby to meet the couple who were adopting the baby.

She left the house that day about 11.30 a.m., and sat on a Bench in the park. Her head was in turmoil. She began to wonder if she was doing the right thing, and the answer came to her straight away: do not give your baby away. It is the wrong thing to do; you will regret it for many years to come.

She jumped up and dashed back to her guest house, but her baby was gone and the rule of the social service is they do not give the name of the people who adopt a baby.

She has cried every day since for what she has done. She prays to God every day that, with His help, she may find her child. She has written a letter to him every day in the hope that, when they find him, that he will understand the reason for her decision.

Rooney, George

I Got Sacked for Being Santa Claus

My name: Rasher Byrne

Age: 65 years

Retired

You might well ask where the name "Rasher" came from. Well, I live in a small basement flat just off O'Connell Street, and there are two families who live on the floors above, and, from time to time, the mothers in the families would say to the children,

"Go down to Mister Byrne and see does he want any messages."

One thing I would often ask them to get me was "a few rashers." Hence, the name "Rashers" was born.

It was a lovely, mid November, day; so I decided to take a walk down O'Connell Street, and just when I was passing a large toy store, I heard a voice calling me. I turned around and I saw this well-dressed man standing in the doorway of the store, and he said to me,

"You have a lovely long beard. Would you like to take the job of doing Santa Claus in the store?"

He then brought me into the shop and showed me the hut where I would be sitting.

"The parcels for the girls are on the left and the parcels for the boys are on the right."

I began to think that things were looking up for Christmas, until, two weeks before Christmas, I just happened to look over at the front window, and I saw there two children with their faces pressed against the window. With a wave of my arm, I indicated for them to come in to me.

I said to them, "Have you been to see Santa Claus yet?"

"No," was their reply; "Our ma does not have any money."

Without another word, I put my hand up and took down two of the biggest parcels I could find. I then said to them,

"Go home and tell your ma that you met Santa Claus today."

The children had just left with a smile on their faces that would be there until after Christmas.

Then, all of a sudden, I heard a voice coming from the stairway. It was the store manager.

"Mr Byrne, I have seen what you did. Do you think I am running a charity shop? You are sacked. Go to the office and collect your wages."

I got sacked for being Santa Claus.

Shaw, Ethel Walker

Mattie and Sammy, the Jack Russell

Story 1

Mattie Lane became homeless when he could no longer pay the rent for his single-bedroom flat.

Each night, he bedded down at about 11.30 in a doorway in Anglesea Street, off Dame Street, and he was lucky that a kind person would sometimes give him a breakfast roll, measuring about 8 inches, which had in it ham, cheese, tomato, scallions and bacon.

One night, after he had cut the roll into 3 pieces, which he would make last to the morning, he saw, staring at him intently, a little white and tan Jack Russell, with a cute face like a pet fox. Being very hungry himself, he only managed to give the dog a tiny crust. Sammy, as he was later named, went away dejected with his little tail down, towards Aston Quay.

The next night, Sammy appeared again, and only received the crumbs that fell from the poor man's lap.

But the third night, wait till you hear what happened! Sammy appeared out of nowhere and Mattie, searching for his pen-knife, took his eye off the ball. Sammy, who was quicker than a cat on a hot tin roof, wasted not a second, and made off with the roll in his mouth, down Anglesea Street speedily, and turned right towards O'Connell Bridge.

Mattie was absolutely raging; jumped up and began running like the hammers of hell after our little friend, swearing and yelling words that I could not repeat. Even though Mattie used to be a very good runner himself, he failed to catch up with Sammy, who could be seen up a lane at the back of a shop enjoying his ill-gotten gains.

The next night, believe it or not, at 11.30, Mattie was preparing to have his first bite when, only five feet away, there was Sammy, courageously and hopefully staring at Mattie.

Mattie, being highly intelligent himself, decided to pull a fast one. He was not going to be robbed a second time. He took out a piece of the ham with his left hand and offered it to Sammy, who carefully came over to receive it. As he was doing so, Mattie grasped Sammy and held him firmly. But the unexpected happened.

Sammy ate the ham with such gusto that he was also licking Mattie's fingers and then jumped and licked his face so much that he, Mattie, was so overwhelmed with all this affection that he said, "OK! You can stay the night beside me in my cardboard box."

That was the beginning of the most loving friendship imaginable.

Story 2

The one thing Mattie dreaded to lose was his mobile phone, and it is well known that some needy people will not avail of the hostels because it is common to be robbed, not only of money, but mobile phones as well.

Sammy was fascinated with Mattie's mobile, and he often turned round to see the dog with it in his mouth.

One day, when Mattie was playing "There goes that train," on his harmonica (on O'Connell Bridge), a crowd of tourists and ordinary people gathered around.

Some said, "He's as good as Don Baker or Mick Jagger of the Rolling Stones."

Suddenly, Sammy growled and jumped up quick as lightning through the crowd. People turned around, to see the terrier pursuing a young man who was running as fast as Usain Bolt across into Westmoreland Street. He had Mattie's mobile in his right hand, but, when he saw all eyes were on him; and Sammy had caught up with him, his little, sharp as razors, teeth in his ankle, he yelled and dropped the mobile.

Sammy was back in no time at all with the mobile phone in his mouth, and placed it in the lap of his beloved new owner.

A great cheer went up and they all clapped.

Story 3

People liked Mattie; and Mattie was always interested in people, and life did not turn him into a cynic. He'd often say, "There's a great big world out there," or "Life is for living."

One evening, around 7 pm, he sat down with his sleeping bag and bits and pieces in Merchant Arch, near the Halfpenny Bridge. Sammy kept very close and often people, especially dog-lovers, would admire him, and say, "I would love to be able to have a dog again."

Jack Russells are very popular.

He took out his book, *Staring at Lakes,* by Michael Harding, and reflected, "Even he, who is a well-known author and probably not short of money, is suffering from depression."

What made Mattie very sad was the fact that his best friend, Tony, had to emigrate. His eyes welled up with tears. Sammy was in the crook of his arm and, before Mattie attempted to wipe them away, Sammy got up on his hind legs and licked and licked and licked his face.

I am convinced that the sight of Mattie weeping tugged at the heart strings of his little dog.

At about 2 a.m., having dozed off for a while, he awoke and got the shock of his life to find no sign of Sammy. In a flash, Mattie thought he couldn't bear it if he disappeared out of his life, even thought he was with him for less than a week.

Suddenly, there was a screech, and Mattie looked down Anglesea Street, to see a black cat running for his life, and who was pursuing it only Sammy!

Mattie heaved a deep sigh of relief, and the two pals slept a sleep of peace.

Story 4

One afternoon around 4 o'clock, on O'Connell Bridge, when

people were beginning to go home, a young man, about twenty-eight, approached Mattie. He had a very good guitar under his arm.

The first thing he did was admire the Jack Russell. He said, "Dogs' Rescue are frantically looking for homes for unwanted dogs."

Mattie started to play Louis Armstrong's *"It's a Wonderful World"* on the harmonica. The young man, Jimmy, who was an exceptionally good guitarist, with a rich melodious baritone voice, played along. The music was so rich and harmonious; you could see people were visibly moved. It was so joyful and sad, people didn't try to hide their feelings. This was better than the X Factor, people said.

Then they played and sang *Amazing Grace,* followed by *Danny Boy.*

Then Jimmy noticed Sammy licking Mattie's leg and wouldn't stop. Jimmy looked down, and couldn't believe what he saw. Mattie's leg was ulcerated.

"Merciful Hour, Mattie, if you don't have it seen to, it could get worse."

Mattie said that it would be a problem going to hospital. "Who'd mind Sammy?"

Jimmy said, "I'll tell you what. My mother has a little Jack Russell, called Freddie. He, like Sammy, is a great character, and everyone loves him. Mammy would never be without a dog. My dad is the same. I'll ask her if she would mind Sammy. I know she won't refuse. Freddie was found at the side of the road in Naas and we adopted him."

PROBLEM SOLVED.

Shaw, Ethel Walker

The Narrow Door

I wandered down strange pathways to Perdition.
I stole a backward glance at those behind.
My mother stretched her arms in sad beseeching,
As I travelled down those dark and eerie ways.
They told me I should search for Peace and Beauty.
It seems I took a wrong and doleful turn.
As angel after angel shed her tears,
The music was the saddest that I've known.

They whispered that my soul was nearly captured;
My only chance was through the Narrow Door.
I saw a beckoning light, far in the distance,
And left behind their cries for evermore.
Before I reached this light, I saw a Demon,
A most horrific being to behold,
He tried to halt my footsteps on that journey
But some great Force just wrenched me from his hold.

The agony of straining through
That straight and narrow door,
As if limb from limb were torn from me!
I lay prostrate on the floor.
My pain-racked ribs could hardly move;
I drew a breath once more,
That lovely air, so fresh, so pure,
My soul began to soar.

I glided through the gentle air
Over shimmering, sparkling waters,

To a new land rich in flowers
Of pink and silver orchids.
Floating by, like fleecy clouds,
Were faces of my friends
Who passed away some years ago
From shores of distant lands.

The presence of my King of Kings
Was all around my Heaven,
With smiles of peace, He greeted me,
And tender sweet caresses.
The magic music played and played;
My Scroll of Life unfolded;
An angel took me by the hand
And led me home un-scolded.

Shaw, Ethel Walker

The Fate of Fred, the Bantam

When Tim McCarthy and Katie O'Brien became engaged, they decided that when they got married, they would keep hens. They had both lived all their lives in the country, so, when they came to live in a Dublin suburb, they were delighted to find that, not only was there a large back garden, but, beyond it was a vast expanse of lovely green fields, in which cattle grazed.

Tim was a keen gardener, and often on a Summer's day Katie felt very happy as she looked out of the kitchen window at the colourful scene of flowers and shrubs, while their children played with Sandy, a golden Labrador and Pedro, a smooth-haired fox terrier. Tim built a small henhouse himself, and fenced in a sizeable part of the garden for a hen-run. Then he wrote to his old friend Cissy Fagan to send him up by rail a few of her very high-class Rhode Island Reds and white Wyandottes. There was some excitement the day they arrived at Kingsbridge Station, a dozen pullets, in all, carefully placed in lightweight timber boxes.

The children took a great interest, as they watched the pullets developing into fully grown hens, laying eggs, which were tiny at first, but getting larger by the week. They even gave names to the hens like Miss Prim, Clara, Báinín, Hickety-Pickety and Fussy Red-feathers.

The names were nicely printed, with colourful paint, on the outside of the laying boxes, which were made very comfortable with fresh yellow straw.

The McCarthys soon discovered that hen-watching was very therapeutic.

Any day that was fine, Katie sat on a deckchair in the garden, dividing her time between reading a romantic novel and gazing at the scene around her. It reminded her of the farmhouse near Lisdoonvarna, in the heart of County Clare, where she used to live as a child. Sometimes she would just close her eyes and listen to the humming of bees and other peaceful sounds of Summer. Nothing made her feel more contented than the low crooning and crowing of the hens gently chirping and picking for worms or busily making sand-baths.

She agreed with the poet who wrote "one is nearer God's heart in a garden than anywhere else on earth."

But this peaceful state was not destined to last very long. Tim and Katie were dismayed to see that the hens had developed a cannibalistic streak of picking and eating the feathers off one another.

Perhaps there was something lacking in their diet of *Layers' Mash* and greens.

It got so bad that, in no time at all, the once beautiful chickens were to be seen chasing all over the run with baldy bottoms and scrawny necks, except for one lady, who presumably was the "queen." Tim, thinking it was high time to do something about it, decided to get a bantam cock, as these creatures had a wonderful reputation for keeping order in the hen run.

One day the children pointed out an advertisement in the Poultry Column of a Dublin paper. It read: "Bantam cock and hen for sale £5. Call to The Beeches, Woodbrook Lawn, Greystones."

Tim, Katie and the five children, aged from four to ten, piled into the family car and hastily headed for this address. They proceeded up the tree-lined drive to a large, old-fashioned, picturesque house.

When they rang the bell, the door was opened by a Mrs. Reddington, a big, cheerful, generous-looking woman, who wore a large sloppy white dress. She was red-faced and quite overweight. She welcomed everyone as if they were her own relations and asked the name of each of the children in turn saying something kind at each introduction, such as "Rosemary, what a nice name," and "I also have a son called Tony."

She informed them that they had decided to part with the bantams, as her children were now "into" canaries.

She introduced them to her husband, a tall, dignified-looking man with the appearance of a brigadier. He nodded, smiled and quietly smoked his pipe.

They were led through the hall and kitchen and out into the sunny back garden.

Then they caught sight of the bantam cock with his fiery red comb, russet and black plumage, and magnificent tail of green, orange, red and black feathers.

His spouse was a sweet little bantam-hen that chirped

merrily. She had black feathers but, beauty-wise, she wouldn't hold a candle to her handsome husband. The Reddlngtons had named them Fred and Henrietta.

Now, the fun was about to begin – when it was decided that Tim and Mrs. Reddington would round them up. Mrs. Reddington suggested: "You go that way, Mr. McCarthy, and I'll go this way." Tim turned to the children and ordered "Keep back now, all of you. And not a word!"

Mr. Reddington stood there patiently smoking his pipe, but his solemn face was a poor disguise for the devilment in his eyes.

Tim and Mrs. Reddington didn't seem to be making any progress catching the bantams, and all you could see was her billowing white skirts and her anxious red face, puffing and blowing, while she and Tim ran all over the garden in hot pursuit. The bantams screeched their heads off madly every time they nearly got caught.

The children would have given anything to assist in the chase, so fully convinced were that they would be more successful than their elders. But they were told to stay exactly where they were.

Suddenly, the pursuers spied Fred behind a low bush, and both dashed in his direction at the same time. Tim, however, had a misunderstanding with his feet, tripped and fell to the ground and Mrs R landed on top of him like a parachute. There was an unmerciful scream from the escaping bantam.

As Tim picked himself up, his wife was fully aware of what

he was muttering and, as you may have guessed, it is unprintable. Mr Reddington exploded with laughter and had to hold on to a tree for support. The children sniggered uncontrollably, thinking it the most comical and undignified scene they had ever witnessed.

Finally, when everyone was allowed to co-operate, the bantams were caught by two of the boys, Tony and Fionn. As they were departing for home, Tim said: "I'll bet they were only too glad to get rid of those cursed blighters."

When they reached home there was an air of excitement, as everyone wondered what the reaction of the hens would be to the newcomers.

But, as expected, Fred took over the whole joint with cocky determination! That very afternoon, while the family were sitting at the table in the kitchen enjoying lunch, four-year-old Seamus couldn't wait to finish his meal quickly enough in order to go out again to inspect the hens. In a few seconds he could be seen running down the garden path as fast as his little legs could carry him, calling frantically "come twickly, come twickly, the bantam jumped up on top of a hen. He's pecking at her hair and holding her with his paws!"

It only took a very short time to discover that Fred was going to rule his harem with the utmost discipline! Also, egg production was very good and the problem of feather-plucking was solved now that they had other things to think about! However he was so possessive about the hens that no one could go into the henhouse in comfort to collect the eggs, or bring in the food. If anyone was wearing sandals, be would peck at their toes and he often flew up and pecked Tim on the back of the hand. Standing there menacingly, be would take a sideways run at anybody when they entered the run. He looked very determined with his mean-looking beady eyes.

The McCarthys tolerated this state ·of affairs for about two months, but, finally, had a round-table conference about the future of Fred.

It was decided he was far too good at his job, a cursed little know-all, and, since he made life hell for everyone, it was agreed to have him fired. He was given as a "gift" to the family of a friend of Tim's by the name of Nattie Crowly, a farmer.

Fred was delivered to Mrs. Crowly one afternoon while Nattie was safely at work, knowing nothing of what was going on. To make doubly sure that Fred wouldn't be landed back on the door-step, the McCarthys took the phone off the hook at night, and Tim avoided Nattie in the pub for a week.

A true story, but names have been changed.

Made in the USA
Monee, IL
04 March 2020